FIDELER SOCIAL STUDIES

World Cultures   (Basic Area Studies)

The people, geography, and history of six world regions.

(Individual books)

CHINA	SOUTHEAST ASIA
JAPAN	AFRICA
INDIA	SOVIET UNION

American Neighbors

The people, geography, and history of Canada, Mexico, Caribbean Lands, and South America. Depth Studies.

The United States

The people, geography, and history of the United States. The Northeast, The South, Midwest and Great Plains, The West . Depth Studies.

Inquiring About Freedom

United States history. Depth Studies of the "freedom" concepts that built our nation.

Contributors to Africa

JOHN N. PADEN
  Professor of Political Science
  Director, Program of African Studies
  Northwestern University
  Evanston, Illinois

G. ETZEL PEARCY
  Chairman, Department
    of Geography
  California State University
  Los Angeles, California

SILENCE M. ANDREWS   DEBORAH R. HENDRICKS

ROBERT H. BAUER   MARGARET FISHER HERTEL

DEBORAH J. BOLT   MARY MITUS

BETTY-JO BUELL   BEV J. ROCHE

MARGARET S. DeWITT   MARY JANE SACK

RAYMOND E. FIDELER   ALICE W. VAIL

MARIANNE FRIEDL   JOANNA VAN ZOEST

AUDREY WITHAM

AFRICA

Benjamin E. Thomas, Editor

Dr. Benjamin E. Thomas is Professor Emeritus of Geography at the University of California, Los Angeles. He is internationally known as a geographer and as the author of books and articles on Africa. Dr. Thomas is a member of the Association of American Geographers.

William D. Allen, Author

William D. Allen has traveled widely in Africa. His knowledge of this continent has enabled him to show his readers the land and the people of Africa in a vivid and interesting manner.

Jerry E. Jennings, Author

Jerry E. Jennings is a writer and editor of textbooks for young people. A graduate of Michigan State University, Mr. Jennings continued his education at Columbia University.

COPYRIGHT 1986, THE FIDELER COMPANY

Earlier edition copyright, 1981

LIBRARY OF CONGRESS CATALOG CARD NUMBER: 85-81418
ISBN: 0-88296-144-6

THE FIDELER COMPANY   GRAND RAPIDS, MICHIGAN

CONTENTS

Maps and Special Features

AFRICA

An Overview of Africa

The second largest continent. Africa is a huge continent that lies in the Eastern Hemisphere* of our earth. It is bordered by the Atlantic Ocean on the west and the Indian Ocean on the east. To the north is the Mediterranean Sea, which separates Africa from Europe. On the northeast, the Red Sea and the Suez Canal* separate Africa from Asia. (See map on page 5.)

Africa is more than three times as large as our country, the United States. It is larger than any other continent on earth except Eurasia.*

A land of great variety. In a continent as large as Africa, it is not surprising to find different kinds of land and climate. The equator* passes through the central part of this continent. As a result, the weather in much of Africa is warm or hot the year around. However, there are great differences in rainfall. Some parts of Africa are very dry, while others are very wet. In some areas, there are broad grasslands with scattered clumps of trees. In other places, there are dense forests or barren deserts. Africa also has rugged mountains whose tops are always covered with snow.

Africa is rich in natural resources. It has large deposits of copper, gold, and many other minerals. It also has large forests and valuable fishing grounds. There are many rivers that can be used to provide waterpower for industry. However, many of Africa's rich resources have not yet been developed.

The home of many different peoples. About 550 million people live in Africa today. This is more than twice as many people as there are in the United States. Since Africa is so large, however, it is not at all crowded. In fact, many parts of Africa are almost empty of people. *See Glossary

In an African village. The women in this picture are pounding manioc* to make flour. Most of Africa's people live in small villages like this one. Because the weather is usually warm, household activities are often carried on outdoors.

2

A continent with an exciting past. Africa has a long and rich history. Many scientists believe that the first human beings lived in Africa more than two million years ago. One of the world's first great civilizations grew up in Africa before 3000 B.C. This was the civilization of ancient Egypt. Later, Africa became the home of several powerful kingdoms that were famous for their wealth and learning.

About five hundred years ago, people from Europe began coming to Africa. At first, they settled only along the coast. As time passed, they gradually pushed their way inland. By the late 1800's, most of Africa was under the control of European nations.

A land of many young nations. The people of Africa did not like being ruled by foreigners. They began struggling for their independence, and they finally won it. In 1950 there were only four independent countries in Africa. Today this continent has more than fifty independent nations.

Africa's people face many problems. Independence did not solve many of the problems facing the people of Africa. Today, most African countries are very poor. There is much political unrest. Many African farmers use old-fashioned tools and methods. Poor soil and lack of rainfall cause crop failures. The population is increasing at an alarming rate.There are not enough roads, schools, or hospitals. There is little modern industry.

These problems keep many of Africa's people from meeting all of their basic needs. (See page 95.) Later in this book, you will discover more about Africa's problems and what is being done to help solve them.

Casablanca is a large, modern city in Morocco. (See map, page 5.) Today most African cities are growing rapidly. Why is this so?

Africa's people are divided into many groups. These groups speak different languages and follow very different ways of life. Most Africans still live in small villages scattered through the countryside. They earn their living mainly by farming. There are few large cities in Africa at present.But Africa's cities are growing rapidly. Each year, thousands of people leave their farms and move to the cities in search of better-paying jobs.

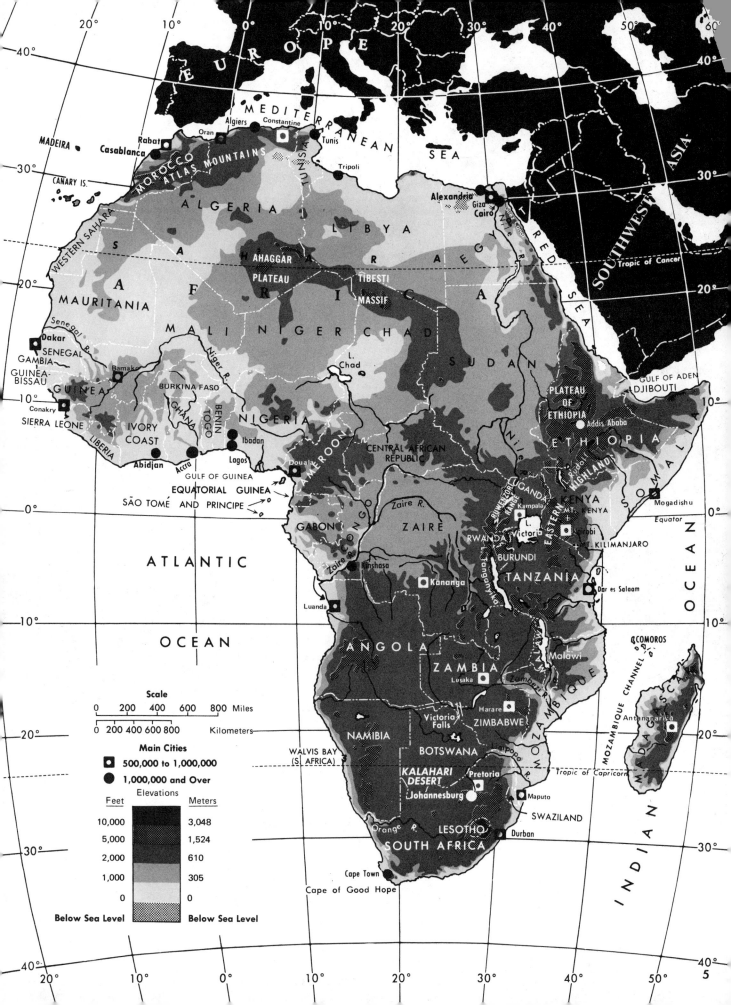

EUROPE

20° 10° 0° 10° 20° 30° 40° 50° 60°

40°

MADEIRA

CANARY IS.

MEDITERRANEAN SEA

Rabat Algiers Constantine
Casablanca Oran Tunis
MOROCCO ATLAS MOUNTAINS Tripoli
ALGERIA LIBYA
WESTERN SAHARA S A H A R A
AHAGGAR PLATEAU TIBESTI
MASSIF
MAURITANIA MALI NIGER CHAD
SENEGAL Senegal R. Niger R. L. Chad
Dakar
GAMBIA Bamako BURKINA FASO SUDAN
GUINEA-BISSAU GHANA BENIN TOGO NIGERIA
Conakry IVORY COAST Ibadan
SIERRA LEONE Accra Lagos
LIBERIA Abidjan GULF OF GUINEA

Alexandria Giza Cairo
EGYPT Suez Canal Nile RED SEA
Tropic of Cancer

PLATEAU OF ETHIOPIA DJIBOUTI GULF OF ADEN
Addis Ababa
ETHIOPIA

EQUATORIAL GUINEA
SÃO TOMÉ AND PRINCIPE
CAMEROON
GABON CONGO ZAIRE R. ZAIRE
Douala CENTRAL AFRICAN REPUBLIC UGANDA KENYA
Kinshasa Zaire R. RUWENZORI RANGE Rudolf Mogadishu
RWANDA L. Victoria Nairobi MT. KENYA
Kananga BURUNDI EASTERN MT. KILIMANJARO
Luanda TANZANIA Dar es Salaam

ATLANTIC OCEAN

SOUTHWEST ASIA

INDIAN OCEAN

Equator 0°

ANGOLA ZAMBIA Lusaka Zambezi R. MALAWI Malawi COMOROS
Victoria Falls Harare ZIMBABWE MOZAMBIQUE MADAGASCAR Antananarivo
NAMIBIA BOTSWANA Limpopo R. MOZAMBIQUE CHANNEL
WALVIS BAY (S. AFRICA) KALAHARI DESERT Pretoria Tropic of Capricorn
Johannesburg Maputo SWAZILAND
Orange R. LESOTHO Durban
SOUTH AFRICA
Cape Town
Cape of Good Hope

INDIAN OCEAN

Scale
0 200 400 600 800 Miles
0 200 400 600 800 Kilometers

Main Cities
◨ 500,000 to 1,000,000
● 1,000,000 and Over

Elevations
Feet Meters
10,000 3,048
5,000 1,524
2,000 610
1,000 305
0 0
Below Sea Level Below Sea Level

5

Part 1
Land and Climate

The huge continent of Africa has many contrasting land features, as well as climates that differ greatly from one region to another. As you do research in this book, try to discover ways in which land features and climate in Africa affect the following:

- where the people live
- kinds of shelter
- types of clothing worn by different peoples in Africa
- vegetation found in different parts of the continent
- farming
- transportation

Mount Kilimanjaro in eastern Africa is the continent's highest mountain. What are some of Africa's other main land features? In which parts of Africa are they located?

1 Land

Most of Africa is a vast plateau.* In some places, this plateau is high and rugged. In other places, it is flat or gently rolling. Africa has only a few small ranges of mountains. Along the African coasts are level lowlands. Most of these extend inland for only a few miles.

The Sahara. The vegetation map on page 16 shows that more than one third of Africa is made up of deserts. The best known of these deserts is the Sahara, in northern Africa. It stretches all the way from the Atlantic Ocean to the Red Sea. The Sahara is the largest desert in the world. Parts of it are covered by ridges of sand that have been piled up by the wind. In other places, the ground is covered with fine pebbles. There are also mountains and rocky highlands. In the drier parts of this huge wasteland, it is almost impossible for plants or animals to live.

Scattered through the Sahara are green, fertile areas of land called oases. These areas are watered by springs, streams, or wells. Some oases are so large that thousands of people make their homes there.

*See Glossary

An Algerian town in the Sahara. In some parts of this great desert, there are areas called oases. Here, springs, streams, or wells provide water for trees and other plants to grow. Write a paragraph describing what you think it would be like to live in the town shown below.

The Atlas Mountains. In the far northwestern part of Africa are the rugged Atlas Mountains. (See map on page 5.) They lie between the Sahara and the sea. Some of the peaks here rise more than thirteen thousand feet above sea level. A few are covered with snow most of the year.

The Nile Valley. Flowing through the northeastern part of Africa is the longest river in the world. This is the Nile River. The map on page 5 shows that the Nile flows northward from Lake Victoria to the Mediterranean Sea. At the mouth of the river is a low, flat delta.* Farther south, a green strip of irrigated land extends for hundreds of miles on both sides of the river. The desert sands come to the very edge of these irrigated fields. The Nile Delta and the northern part of the Nile Valley are among the most fertile farming areas in the world. Millions of people make their homes here.

The grasslands of northern Africa. South of the Sahara, vast grasslands stretch for thousands of miles across the continent. (See the vegetation map on page 16.) In some places, these grasslands look like the western prairies of the United States. Scattered through the grasslands are clumps of bushes and many small trees. Some parts of the grasslands are used for grazing cattle, sheep, and goats. In other places, the grass has been plowed up in order to grow crops such as corn, peanuts, and cotton.

The tropical rainforest. South of the grasslands, near the center of Africa, is a great forest of tall trees. This kind of forest is called a tropical rainforest, because it grows only where the cli-

Africa's grasslands provide pasture for antelope and other wild animals. List some of the ways in which human beings use the grasslands.

mate is hot and damp. The Zaire* (Congo) River flows through the heart of this region. Many smaller rivers empty into the mighty Zaire. Along the riverbanks are dense jungles, with vines twisting between the trees.

The Great Rift Valley. To the east of the rainforest are several large valleys. They are parts of a huge split in the earth's surface called the Great Rift

Valley. (See map below.) The Great Rift Valley extends more than four thousand miles from southwestern Asia to southeastern Africa. It is so large it can be seen from the moon. The Red Sea fills one part of the Great Rift Valley. There are many lakes in the branches of the valley that extend through Africa. Among these are Lake Malawi,* Lake Tanganyika,* and Lake Rudolf.

Rugged highlands and towering mountains border parts of the Great Rift Valley in Africa. Rising above one branch of the valley is the Ruwenzori Range. The peaks here are sometimes called the "Mountains of the Moon." East of the valley are Mount Kenya and Mount Kilimanjaro. These are Africa's highest peaks. Mount Kilimanjaro towers nearly twenty thousand feet above sea level.

The Eastern Highlands. An important highland region that borders the Great Rift Valley is the Eastern Highlands. It is a high plateau extending through Ethiopia, Kenya, and Tanzania. (See map on page 5.) Grasslands cover much of the Eastern Highlands. There are also many farms here. The soil and climate in this part of Africa are very good for growing crops.

Southern Africa. In the southern part of Africa are more grasslands and forests. (See the vegetation map on page 16.) There is also another desert, called the Kalahari. Most of the land in southern Africa is higher in elevation than the land farther north. The Drakensberg Mountains in Lesotho and the Republic of South Africa rise more than eleven thousand feet above sea level.

Great Rift Valley

Murchison Falls is on the Nile River in Uganda. From here the river flows mainly northward for more than 3,000 miles to empty into the Mediterranean Sea. The Nile is the world's longest river. Do research to find ways in which the Nile is important to people who live in its valley.

In the tropical rainforest of central Africa the air is moist and hot. Why is the climate hot in this part of Africa? Do research in other sources to discover what kinds of vegetation grow in the tropical rainforest.

2 Climate

A Problem To Solve
Like most lands that lie near the equator, central Africa has a hot climate. However, even in the hot lands, or tropics, there are important differences in climate from one place to another. Why is the climate milder and drier in some parts of the tropics than it is in others? To solve this problem, you will need to make several hypotheses. In forming your hypotheses, you may want to consider how climate is affected by each of the following:
1. distance from the equator
2. elevation of the land
3. surface features of the land
4. distance from the ocean
Refer to pages 4-5 of the Skills Manual for help in finding additional information in other sources.

See Skills Manual, "Solving Problems"

In much of Africa, the weather is hot throughout the year. The map on page 5 helps to explain why. It shows us that the equator passes through the central part of the continent. Lands near the equator are never tipped away from the sun as are lands that lie closer to the North Pole or the South Pole. Since the sun is almost directly overhead all year long, the weather in central Africa is always hot, except in the mountains. Of course there are differ-

ences in climate in a continent as huge as Africa. Let's take a trip to see some of these differences for ourselves.

Climate in the tropical rainforest. First we board a plane which takes us to the tropical rainforest region of Africa. (See vegetation map on page 16.) Below us we see a blanket of green trees. Our pilot says that trees grow more than one hundred feet tall in the tropical rainforest. They are so close together that sunlight seldom reaches the ground.

When we land and leave our plane, we can tell why this region is heavily forested. The air is so hot and moist that plants grow very rapidly. This part of Africa has no cold weather, for it is very close to the equator. The weather is always hot, and rain falls nearly every day. The wettest months of the year are April and October.

Climate in the grasslands. As we travel northward by car through the tropical rainforest, we notice that the land becomes less wooded. Instead of dense forests, we begin to see tall grass and scattered trees. We have reached the grasslands.

Our guide tells us that most of the grasslands receive less rainfall than the tropical rainforest. Most of the rain comes in summer. The weather here is hot the year around, for this region is not far from the equator.

Climate in the desert. As we travel still farther north, we notice that the countryside begins to look very dry and dusty. We are approaching the great Sahara. When we reach the desert, the burning rays of the sun, the hot wind, and the glittering sand are nearly unbearable. Almost no rain falls here. During the day, hot, dry winds blow southwestward over the Sahara. They swallow up almost all moisture. When the sun sets, however, the temperature drops. It may fall as much as fifty degrees during the night. Rocks sometimes crack from such rapid temperature change. Desert travelers we pass wear long, loose robes to protect themselves from the heat and cold.

Physical Needs

See pages 95-96

A traveler and his camel crossing the Sahara, the great desert of northern Africa. What type of clothing do desert travelers wear? Why do they need this type of clothing? In spite of the harsh climate of the Sahara, some people make their homes in this part of Africa. Do research to discover how these people meet their need for water, food, clothing, and shelter.

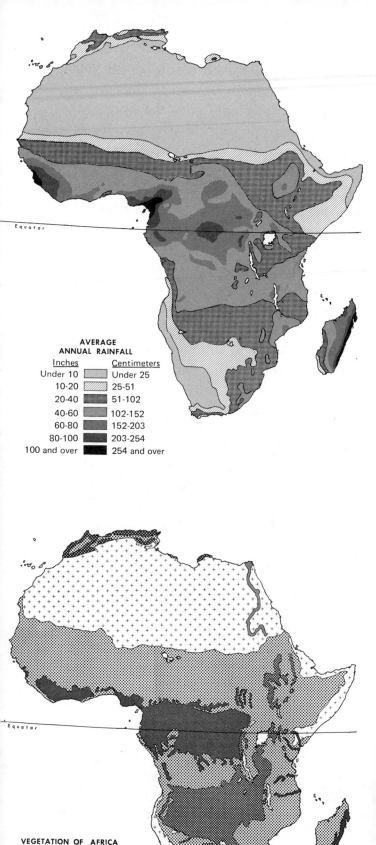

AVERAGE
ANNUAL RAINFALL

Inches		Centimeters
Under 10		Under 25
10-20		25-51
20-40		51-102
40-60		102-152
60-80		152-203
80-100		203-254
100 and over		254 and over

VEGETATION OF AFRICA

Desert and Semidesert
Grassland With Some Bush and Trees
Mediterranean and Cape Forest and Thicket
Forest With Some Grassland
Rainforest
Nile Valley

Learning From Maps

Answer the following questions by studying the maps on this page and comparing them with the map on page 113.

1. How much rainfall do desert and semi-desert areas receive each year? What type of farming or grazing activity is carried on in these areas?

2. What is the main kind of vegetation that grows in areas where there are more than sixty inches of rainfall a year?

3. What is the main kind of vegetation that grows in areas where there are twenty to sixty inches of rainfall a year?

The climate of Africa's northwest coast. We travel northwestward across the desert until we reach the western end of the Atlas Mountains. As we drive northeastward along the strip of fertile land between the mountains and the sea, we pass many vineyards, orchards, and olive groves. Overhead are clear blue skies. The pleasant climate of this part of Africa reminds us of southern California. Summers are hot and dry, and winters are mild and rainy.

The damp winds that blow across the northwest coast of Africa in winter are forced to rise when they reach the Atlas Mountains. High on the cold mountain slopes they lose their moisture in the form of snow. Melted snow from the mountains is an important

Spring in the Atlas Mountains, in Algeria. Melted snow from the Atlas Mountains is an important source of water for people living on the northwest coast of the African continent. Mountain streams provide water for the irrigation of orchards, vineyards, and fields of wheat, barley, and oats.

source of water for the people who live on the coast.

The climate of the Eastern Highlands. Now we board an airplane and fly southeastward to the Eastern Highlands. (See map on page 5.) The Eastern Highlands are so high above sea level that the climate is cool and refreshing. Europeans and Americans feel very much at home here. One of our presidents, Theodore Roosevelt, said that this part of Africa reminded him of the state of Montana.

The climate in the Eastern Highlands is well suited to farming. From late in March until early in June, moist winds from the Indian Ocean sweep over the coasts of Kenya and Tanzania. These winds bring the rainfall that is needed by farm crops and grasslands. Fairly heavy rains also occur here in late fall.

The climate of Africa's southern tip. To end our journey, we fly to the Cape of Good Hope* on the southern tip of the continent. The climate here is similar to the climate we found on our visit to Africa's northwest coast. However, because we are south of the equator, the seasons are turned around. The summer months in this part of Africa, as in other lands in the Southern Hemisphere,* are December, January, and February. These months are very dry. Winters in this part of Africa begin in June. The winter months are rainy, but the temperatures are mild. Because the climate is so pleasant, many Europeans have settled here.

*See Glossary

Summertime in Cape Town. In the Republic of South Africa and other lands south of the equator, summer begins in December. Do research in other sources to discover why this is so. (Perhaps you noticed that all of the people at this pool in Cape Town are white. Because South Africa has a system called apartheid,* black people are not allowed to use white recreation areas.)

Desert Lands of the World

About one third of Africa consists of deserts. Desert lands also cover large areas of Asia, Australia, and North America. Choose one of the deserts listed below and compare it with the great Sahara.

the Gobi	the Takla Makań
the Negev	the Mojave

Share your findings with your class in a report that compares the following information about the Sahara and the desert you have chosen.

1. size and land features
2. sources of water
3. temperatures and rainfall

Pages 4-8 of the Skills Manual contain suggestions that will help you find information and write your report.

Investigate the Great Rift Valley

The Great Rift Valley cuts through much of eastern Africa. To learn more about this enormous split in the earth's surface, do research in other sources. Then prepare an oral report to share with your classmates. In your report, you may wish to include information about the following:

1. size and location of the Great Rift Valley
2. how the valley was formed
3. what bodies of water lie in the Great Rift Valley
4. how the land features of the valley affect transportation in Africa

The suggestions on pages 4-9 of the Skills Manual will be helpful in finding information and preparing your report.

Discover Africa's Animals

Photographers and scientists from many countries come to Africa to photograph and study the wild animals that live here. Africa has a great variety of wildlife. Write an interesting report on one of the animals of Africa. Include the following facts in your report:

1. a brief description of the animal
2. the parts of Africa where it lives
3. some of its habits
4. how it adapts to its surroundings

The suggestions on pages 4-8 of the Skills Manual will help you locate information and write a good report. If possible, illustrate your report with pictures.

Explore Wildlife Conservation

The picture at left shows hippopotamuses in Kruger National Park in the Republic of South Africa. This park is one of the largest wildlife reserves* in the world. Other countries in Africa have also established reserves to conserve their wildlife. Prepare for a class discussion on the conservation of wildlife.

The suggestions on pages 4-5 of the Skills Manual will help you locate information. The following questions will guide you in your research and in holding your discussion.

1. Many kinds of animals have become extinct* or nearly extinct. How have natural causes and people's actions destroyed or reduced wildlife?
2. Do you think conservation of wildlife is important? Why? Why not?
3. How does your state attempt to conserve wildlife?

Refer to the suggestions on page 9 of the Skills Manual for a successful discussion.

Use Your Imagination

Imagine that you are a writer for a travel magazine. You have just taken a boat trip on the Nile River in Egypt, from Alexandria to Aswan. Write an article describing your journey. In your article, include answers to the following questions.

1. What interesting sights did you see along the way? Include information about land and water features, plant and animal life, people, cities, and places of historical interest.
2. What kind of weather did you have during your journey?

Do research in this book and other sources to find the information you need. Use your imagination in writing your article, but be sure the information you present is based on facts.

Make a Relief Map of Africa

With a group of your classmates, make a relief map of the African continent. First, find a large map of Africa in an atlas and trace an outline of the continent. Use carbon paper to transfer this outline to a piece of heavy cardboard. Then, using the map on page 5 as a guide, form the highlands and lowlands of Africa with clay. After allowing the clay to dry thoroughly (at least twenty-four hours), paint your relief map with poster paints or tempera. Use different colors to indicate deserts, grasslands, mountains, and rainforests, as well as such features as the Nile Valley and large rivers and lakes. You may also wish to indicate the location of some of Africa's large cities.

Part 2
History and Government

During the long time that people have been living in Africa, vast changes have taken place. Do research to discover what some of these changes have been and why they occurred. As you read, try to answer the following questions.

- How did the early Africans make their living? What happened after farming was introduced?
- Where did the first great civilization in Africa develop? What was this civilization like?
- In what ways was early Africa influenced by the Phoenicians? Romans? Greeks? Arabs?
- What great kingdoms were established in western, central, and eastern Africa? What caused the rise and fall of these kingdoms?
- How did the coming of Europeans affect the people of Africa?
- How has independence from European rule helped to improve the lives of Africans? What new problems has it created?
- What kinds of governments are found in Africa today?

The Temple of Amon-Re at Karnak, Egypt. Egyptians built a great civilization along the Nile River more than five thousand years ago.

3 Africa Long Ago

The early peoples of Africa. People were living in Africa hundreds of thousands of years ago. Because writing had not yet been invented at that time, these early people kept no written records. As a result, little was known about them until the present century. Then scientists called archaeologists began trying to learn more about them. By digging carefully in the earth near caves and in other places where early people might have stayed, archaeologists have uncovered many ancient tools and other objects. These objects help us imagine what life was like in Africa long ago.

Like other early peoples, the early Africans obtained most of their food by hunting and gathering. Usually the men of a community killed giraffes and other animals for food and for skins with which to make clothing. The women and children gathered berries, seeds, and roots.

The early peoples of Africa lived in small groups made up of only a few families. Most groups traveled from

Ancient cave paintings in northern Africa. Although the early peoples of Africa left no written records, cave paintings like these help scientists to imagine what life was like in Africa long ago.

place to place in search of good hunting grounds. The early Africans did not build houses for shelter. However, they sometimes lived in caves or in crude shelters made from tree branches.

Life was difficult and dangerous for the early peoples of Africa. Often the hunters could not find enough food. When this happened, people sometimes died of starvation. Sometimes hunters were killed by wild animals. Since the people of early times knew little about health care, many of them died of diseases. It is not surprising that only a small number of people lived in Africa at this time.

Some of Africa's people became farmers. As time passed, an important change began to take place in the early peoples' way of life. People who had formerly obtained their food by hunting began to grow crops or to raise animals. These were the world's first farmers.

Scientists who study the past are not sure just when or where farming first developed. However, it is believed that farming probably began in the southwestern part of Asia between 8000 and 7000 B.C. Gradually, farming spread from Southwest Asia to the valley of the Nile River and other fertile areas in northern Africa. Farmers here began to grow such crops as wheat, barley, and flax.* They also raised cattle, sheep, and other kinds of livestock.

More than five thousand years ago, people living in the western part of Africa also began to grow crops. They may have learned about farming from the people who lived in northern Africa, or they may have developed the idea by themselves. Since these farmers lived where the weather was usually hot and humid, they grew crops that were well suited to a tropical climate, such as yams* and rice.

Farming brought great changes in people's way of life. When people in Africa became farmers, their way of life changed greatly. By growing crops and raising livestock, people were able to produce a larger and more dependable supply of food than the early hunters. Since there was less chance of starvation, people lived longer and had more children. As a result, the population increased greatly in the parts of Africa where farming had developed.

When people became farmers, they no longer had to travel constantly in

*See Glossary

Making bricks. When the early peoples of Africa became farmers, they had time for developing new skills, such as brickmaking. The picture above shows some of the steps in making bricks.

search of food. In fact, it was necessary for them to remain in one place long enough to plant and harvest their crops. They began to build houses out of mud, grass, and other materials. Gradually, small villages grew up near the fields where the farmers raised their crops.

The early hunters of Africa had spent nearly all their time just searching for food. When people became farmers, however, they did not have to work all year long planting and harvesting their crops. They had some time which they could use to learn new skills and to find better ways of meeting their needs. For example, new and better tools were needed for farming. The people of Af-

rica learned how to make hoes out of stone and wood to prepare the soil for planting. They also learned how to make sharp sickles,* which they used for harvesting their crops.

The early farmers of Africa also developed many new skills. For example, they learned how to spin thread from fibers of wool and flax and how to weave the thread into cloth. They learned how to use clay in making bricks and pottery, and how to use reeds in making baskets and other articles. With these new skills, people were able to make greater use of their natural resources.

As the population of Africa increased, other important changes started to take

The workers in the center, for example, are mixing clay with straw. One of the men above right is using a wooden form to shape the bricks. The worker at top left is laying the bricks in the sun to dry.

place. Powerful kingdoms began to grow up in different parts of the continent. Let us explore the history of some of these kingdoms.

Northern Africa

About seven thousand years ago, the climate of northern Africa was very different from the climate there today. In many areas, there was enough rainfall to allow grass and even trees to grow. Hunters roamed the forests and grasslands in search of wild animals to kill for food. Herders raised sheep, cattle, and other livestock on the broad, grassy plains.

As time passed, the climate of northern Africa grew drier. The rivers that had flowed there for many years eventually disappeared. The trees and grass withered and died, and much of northern Africa turned into a desert that is now called the Sahara. (See page 8.)

The people in the dry areas of northern Africa found it more and more difficult to obtain the food and water they needed. Gradually, they began moving to certain areas where more water was available. Some of these people moved into the valley of the Nile River, while other people settled along the Mediterranean coast. Still others moved southward.

Farming in the Nile Valley long ago. Early people who settled in the Nile Valley began to grow crops such as barley and wheat. Why was the land in this part of Africa well suited to farming?

The Nile Valley

The valley of the Nile River became a productive farming area. When people first came to the Nile Valley, much of the land there was covered with jungles and swamps. Gradually, the people who lived there cleared away the jungles and drained the water off the land. They laid out fields and began to grow crops such as barley and wheat.

The Nile Valley was extremely well suited to farming. Because most of the land was level, it could be cultivated fairly easily with simple farm tools. Although the climate was very dry, the Nile River provided all the water farmers needed for irrigating their crops. In addition, the river contained much soil that had washed down from the highlands of eastern Africa. (See map on page 5.) Each year, the Nile overflowed its banks and deposited a new layer of rich soil on the land. As a result, the land could be farmed year after year without becoming less fertile. The warm sunshine, the rich soil, and the water from the river helped the farmers in the Nile Valley to produce large amounts of crops.

The people of the Nile Valley learned new ways to meet their needs. Because harvests were so plentiful in the Nile Valley, not all the people there had to work as farmers in order to produce enough food for everyone. Some people were free to do other kinds of work. For example, certain people who were skilled in making things with their hands became craft workers. They produced such articles as cloth and pottery, which they gave to farmers in exchange for the food they needed. Other people became merchants, priests, or soldiers.

As people began to specialize in doing certain kinds of work, they developed new ways of using natural resources. For example, they learned how to produce metals such as copper and bronze* from ores* that they dug out of the earth. These metals could be used in making many different kinds of tools and weapons. Metal tools were generally stronger and more useful than tools made out of stone. People in the Nile Valley raised flax and used the fibers from this plant to weave cloth. They made boats and other articles from reeds that grew along the Nile. Clay from the riverbanks was used in making fine pottery.

The people of the Nile Valley could not obtain all the goods they needed in their own area, so they traded with people in other lands. Since there were no longer any forests in the Nile Valley, wood was brought from Lebanon, in Southwest Asia. Copper ore came from the Sinai Peninsula. (See map on page 33.) Gold, incense,* ivory, and other goods came from tropical lands farther south in Africa. In return for all these goods, the people of the Nile Valley sup-plied the people of neighboring lands with products such as wheat, papyrus,* and cloth.

Although goods were sometimes carried across the desert on donkeys, most goods were transported by boat. The Nile River was an excellent transportation route. While the river flowed from south to north, the winds in the Nile Valley usually blew from north to south. Sailboats could travel southward with the help of the wind, and then return northward by drifting downstream with the current. This made it very easy to travel from one part of the Nile Valley to another.

As time passed, the Nile Valley became densely populated. The vegetation map on page 16 helps to show why this was true. Although the Nile Valley extends for hundreds of miles from south to north, it is very narrow. On each side of the valley is barren desert land. Since the people who lived in the Nile Valley could not spread out into neighboring areas as the population increased, the valley became more and more crowded. The people of the Nile Valley found that they had to cooperate closely in order to avoid conflicts and to meet their needs successfully.

Powerful kings ruled over the Nile Valley. When the Nile Valley was first settled, the people who lived there belonged to many different ethnic* groups. Gradually some of the groups joined with others, and the stronger groups conquered those that were less powerful. About 3100 B.C., all of the Nile Valley was brought under the rule of a single, mighty king. This was the beginning of the great kingdom that we know as Egypt.

The early kings of Egypt were extremely powerful. They could make laws for the kingdom all by themselves. All of the other people in the kingdom had to obey the king's laws and commands without question.

There were several reasons why the Egyptian kings had so much power. In the first place, the people of Egypt knew that if there were wars or fighting of any kind, their farms and villages might be destroyed. They wanted a strong ruler who could prevent wars and keep order.

Egypt's system of agriculture also encouraged the development of strong rulers. Because little rain fell in the Nile Valley, farmers had to irrigate their crops. Many canals were needed to carry water from the Nile River to the fields. In order to build the canals, large numbers of workers were required. A strong ruler could make sure that enough workers were available and that they all worked together on these irrigation projects.

The Nile River helped the Egyptian rulers to maintain their power. Since the valley of the Nile is very narrow, messengers traveling up and down the river by boat could keep the ruler informed about everything that happened in the kingdom.

There was another reason why the Egyptian rulers became so powerful. The people of Egypt believed that their rulers were gods. Therefore, they thought it was their religious duty to obey all their commands and to provide them with everything that they needed.

Egypt became the home of a great civilization. The Egyptians were among the first people anywhere in the world to create a great civilization. Many of the ideas and skills developed by the ancient Egyptians still influence our ways of living today.

The early Egyptians were very skillful builders. They built huge pyramids* from blocks of stone to serve as burial places for their rulers. Some of the pyramids that are standing today are about 4,500 years old. The Egyptians also built many huge temples and palaces. Some of these buildings were decorated with statues of the Egyptian rulers, many times larger than life-size. On the walls of some of the buildings were beautiful paintings.

The Great Sphinx and a pyramid near Cairo are examples of the magnificent building skills of the ancient Egyptians. What are some other important ideas and skills these people developed?

The early Egyptians were among the first people in the world to develop a system of writing. At first, they drew pictures to represent different objects and ideas. Later they also developed symbols to represent some of the sounds that a person makes when he or she speaks. Many of the letters in our own alphabet have been developed from the symbols used by the Egyptians long ago.

Several important discoveries in science and mathematics were made by people in ancient Egypt. By keeping track of the yearly flooding of the Nile River and studying the movements of a bright star known as Sirius, the Egyptians were able to develop a fairly accurate calendar. This helped them to know when to plant and harvest their crops. The Egyptians also worked out some of the rules of geometry* in order to measure the size of their fields. These and other discoveries helped the Egyptians to have a better way of life.

The early Egyptians had certain religious beliefs that are shared by millions of people today. For example, they believed that every person has a soul that continues to live on after death. The Egyptians also believed that good deeds would be rewarded and evil deeds punished in the next life.

Egypt was often threatened by invaders from other lands. Sometimes the entire country was under foreign rule. In spite of these troubles, however, the kingdom of Egypt lasted for almost three thousand years.

The kingdom of Kush was rich and powerful. Another great kingdom that developed in the Nile Valley was Kush. It lay to the south of Egypt, in what is now the country of Sudan.

Long before Kush developed into a kingdom, the people who lived in that part of the Nile Valley were carrying on trade with the people of Egypt. In about 1500 B.C., the people of Kush were conquered by soldiers from Egypt. Kush remained under Egyptian rule for about five hundred years. During this period, the people of Kush learned much about Egypt's civilization. They began to borrow many ideas and skills from the Egyptians. For example, they learned how to use the Egyptian system of writing and how to construct large temples and pyramids. As time passed, Egypt became less powerful. Finally, the people of Kush were able to break away from Egypt and set up their own kingdom.

While some of the people of Kush were farmers or herders, others earned their living from trade. Adventurous merchants from Kush journeyed hundreds of miles to other parts of Africa to carry on trade. As they traded with their neighbors to the west and south, they passed along many of the ideas and skills they had learned.

Like the Egyptians, the early people of Kush used copper and bronze for making tools and weapons. In about 650 B.C., however, warriors from Southwest Asia invaded the Nile Valley. They brought with them their knowledge of ironmaking. Iron was a stronger and more useful metal than copper or bronze. Although Egypt was lacking in iron ore, there were large deposits of this mineral in Kush. Also, there were forests that could supply wood to use as fuel in smelting* the ore. Gradually the people of Kush began to produce large amounts of iron for export to other countries.

The trade in iron and other goods helped to make Kush wealthy and powerful. A great city called Meroë grew up along the Nile River. In this city were huge pyramids and temples, much like those in Egypt.

By the third century A.D., the power of Kush slowly began to decline. Groups of people from the desert often attacked caravans traveling along the trade routes between Kush and other countries. As a result, Kush lost much of its profitable trade. Also, the population of Kush had grown larger. There was no longer enough good farmland in Kush to supply food for all the people who lived there. Some of the land had been used such a long time for growing crops or grazing cattle that it was no longer fertile.

Meanwhile, a new kingdom called Axum was growing up in what is now the country of Ethiopia. (Compare the map at right with the map on page 5.) About A.D. 350, the people of Axum conquered Kush and destroyed the great city of Meroë. For centuries, Kush was almost forgotten. Then, in the 1800's, archaeologists began to explore the ruins of Meroë and other cities. Through the objects they uncovered, we have been able to learn much about the great kingdom of Kush that flourished in the Nile Valley long ago.

The Mediterranean Coast

People from Asia and Europe ruled over lands along the Mediterranean coast. As the climate in what is now the Sahara became drier, some groups of people moved their livestock northward. They settled along the Mediterranean coast of Africa, where rainfall was more plentiful. As time passed, people from other lands began coming to Africa's Mediterranean coast. Among these people were the Phoenicians, the Greeks, and the Romans.

The Phoenicians. The Phoenicians lived in a small country along the eastern shore of the Mediterranean Sea. (See map below.) They were bold sailors and traders. In their small sailing ships, they made long and dangerous voyages across the Mediterranean Sea to exchange goods with other people. Wherever they went, they established trading posts and colonies. By about 700 B.C., there were many Phoenician colonies along the northern coast of Africa. Others were located in the

Northern Africa in early times. Long ago, great civilizations grew up and large cities were founded in the northern part of Africa.

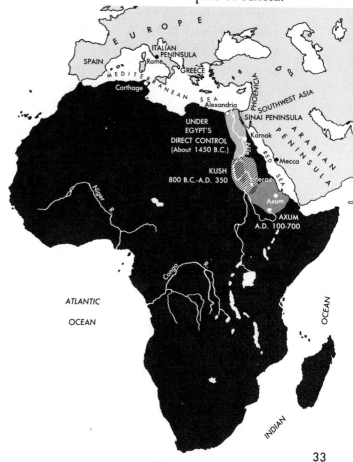

southern part of Spain and on some of the islands of the Mediterranean.

One of the Phoenician settlements in northern Africa, named Carthage, grew into a large and prosperous trading city. By about 600 B.C., Phoenicia had lost much of its power, and Carthage took control of other Phoenician trading posts in the western part of the Mediterranean. In this way, it became the capital of a large trading empire.

The Greeks. The Greeks were another group of people who ruled over parts of northern Africa. Their homeland was a peninsula in the southeastern part of Europe. In 334 B.C., the ruler of Greece, Alexander the Great, led his armies into Southwest Asia. Within a few years, he gained control of a vast empire that extended all the way from northern Africa to India. Along the Mediterranean coast of Egypt, Alexander built a great city to serve as a trading center for his new empire. This city was called Alexandria. Today, about 2,300 years later, Alexandria is the second largest city in Egypt.

The Romans. Long before the time of Alexander the Great, a city was established in the central part of the Italian Peninsula. (See map on page 33.) This city was Rome. The people of Rome were brave fighters who had a strong sense of loyalty to their city. They gradually conquered their neighbors or formed alliances with them. By the middle of the third century B.C., the Romans had gained control of almost all of the peninsula.

At this time, Carthage was a wealthy and powerful city. The people of Carthage feared that Rome might try to conquer part of their empire. The two cities became rivals, and fought three bitter wars for control of the western part of the Mediterranean. In each war, Rome won important victories. Finally, in 146 B.C., the Romans conquered the city of Carthage and destroyed it completely. Most of the people of Carthage were killed or sold into slavery.

The Romans went on to conquer many other lands in Africa, Europe, and Asia. By A.D. 100, they ruled over a great empire that stretched all the way around the Mediterranean Sea.

The Romans brought many changes to the lands they ruled. Before the Roman conquest, the countries around the Mediterranean had often been at war with one another. The Romans established law and order throughout their empire. They were noted for their wise laws and efficient system of government. The Romans were also very skillful in

Roman ruins in Morocco. The Romans brought many changes to northern Africa and to other lands they conquered. What were some of these changes? How do you think they affected the lives of the conquered peoples?

engineering. They built fine roads to connect the different parts of their empire. Large aqueducts carried water from mountain streams to cities and farms. There were beautiful temples and palaces in the cities, as well as huge stadiums where sports events were held. The ruins of many Roman buildings can still be seen in northern Africa today.

As the years passed, the Roman government began to grow weaker. The Romans were no longer as hardworking or as loyal to their empire as their ancestors had been. In the fourth century, the Roman Empire split into two parts, known as the Western Empire and the Eastern Empire.

A short time later, the Western Empire was invaded and destroyed by groups of people who came from northern Europe. These people were fierce and uncivilized. They traveled throughout the Western Empire, attacking the Roman cities and killing people. Many of the skills and ideas of the Romans were forgotten. For this reason, the period of history following the collapse of Rome is often known as the Dark Ages.

The Eastern Empire managed to protect itself from attacks by these invaders. Here, life continued to be fairly peaceful and orderly. For many years, Egypt and some of the other lands in northern Africa remained part of the Eastern Empire.

Arab invaders brought a new way of life to northern Africa. During the seventh century, an important change took place in northern Africa. This area was

A mosque in Tunisia. Arab invaders brought the religion of Islam to northern Africa. In what other ways did they influence the people's way of life in this part of Africa?

invaded by people who came from the Arabian Peninsula, in Southwest Asia. The Arabs, as these people were called, were brave fighters. They had splendid horses and were excellent riders.

The Arabs were inspired by the teachings of a great prophet named Mohammed, who had died in Arabia in 632. These teachings developed into a religion called Islam. According to Islam, there is only one God, and Mohammed is his messenger. The Arabs were extremely loyal to their new religion and wanted to spread it to other countries.

Within a few years, the Arab invaders had swept all the way across northern Africa to the Atlantic Ocean. Some of them even traveled northward into Spain. Wherever the Arabs went, they took their religion and their customs. They also took their language, which is called Arabic.

The Arabs built a number of cities in northern Africa. In these cities were large buildings called mosques, where the followers of Islam could worship God. The Arab rulers also built fine palaces, which were decorated with beautiful works of art.

The Arab invasion had a deep and long-lasting effect on the people's way of life throughout northern Africa. Even today, many people in this area use the Arabic language and follow the religion of Islam.

Africa South of the Sahara

While all of these great events were taking place in northern Africa, many changes were also going on in the part of the continent that lies south of the Sahara. During the time when grasslands covered most of northern Africa (see page 27), people of many different ethnic groups lived on the open plains of the Sahara. After the climate started changing, however, many of these peoples began moving southward in search of a better place to live.

Some of these peoples settled in the grasslands south of the Sahara. Others moved farther south into the rainforests. After these peoples reached their new homelands, some of them probably intermarried with the peoples who were already living there.

Some of the groups of peoples did not settle permanently, however. For many centuries, different groups continued to migrate.* Because of this, much of the history of southern Africa is the story of people moving to new lands and spreading new ideas. One of the important ideas they introduced was the use of iron tools.

As the desert wasteland grew larger, it separated the people living south of the Sahara from the people who settled in the Nile Valley and along the Mediterranean coast. Partly because of this, the people south of the Sahara developed a way of life that was different from that of their neighbors in northern Africa.

Western Africa

Civilizations began to develop in Africa's western grasslands. The people who settled in the grasslands south of the Sahara had vast, open areas in which to hunt and to farm. They were not forced to live as closely together as the people in the north who settled along the coast or in the narrow Nile Valley. When the population in one area became too large for everyone to farm successfully, or when wild animals became too scarce for the hunters, these early peoples would often move on to another area in the grasslands. Sometimes, part of a group would leave to find new lands and build new villages.

The western part of the grasslands had many valuable resources. The people who lived in the western grasslands used certain valuable gifts of nature in meeting their needs. In some areas, the soil was fertile, and there was enough rainfall for growing crops. Farmers in these areas could raise such crops as millet,* sorghum,* and cotton. In areas where there was less rainfall, large herds of cattle and sheep grazed on the tall grass.

The rivers of western Africa were another valuable resource. If we compare the map on page 5 with the vegetation map on page 16, we can see that the Senegal and the Niger rivers flow through the grasslands of western Africa. People traveled up and down these rivers in canoes, carrying goods from one place to another. In some areas, water from the rivers was used for irrigating crops. In addition, the rivers provided fish for food.

There were other valuable natural resources in western Africa. Huge deposits of gold were located in the southern part of the grasslands and in the dense forests along the Gulf of Guinea. Iron ore and copper were also mined in western Africa.

The use of iron weapons helped certain people in western Africa gain power over their neighbors. Some of the people in western Africa learned to make tools and weapons from iron. Possibly they learned the skill of ironmaking before the first century B.C. from traders who came from Kush or from cities along the Mediterranean coast of Africa. With iron tools, the people of western Africa were able to meet their needs more easily. In addition, the people who had iron weapons were able to gain power over those who had weapons made of wood or stone.

Powerful kingdoms developed in the western grasslands. Gradually, the people of western Africa who had iron weapons gained more and more influence over their neighbors. They began to demand tribute* from other groups of people who lived in the grasslands. As their power increased, more land and people came under their control. The leaders of the most powerful groups would appoint officials to collect the tribute. However, they allowed each group of people to govern themselves in their own way.

Between the eighth and fifteenth centuries, some of the peoples of western Africa developed powerful kingdoms. The largest and best-known of these kingdoms were Ghana, Mali, and Songhay. The maps on the opposite page show the area included in each of these kingdoms at the height of its power. Ghana, the first of the three to become powerful, was a wealthy and civilized country at a time when most of Europe was still in the Dark Ages.

Trade helped the kingdoms in the western grasslands become large and prosperous. The people of the western grasslands carried on much trade with one another to obtain the goods they needed. They also traded with people in lands far to the north and south.

Two of the most important products traded by people in western Africa were gold and salt. As you have discovered, there were huge gold deposits in the southern part of the grasslands. However, there was very little salt in this area. In order to stay healthy, all people need salt in their diet. The nearest salt deposits of any size were in the Sahara. The people who lived in this area were glad to send some of their salt to the people who lived in the grasslands in exchange for gold. In this way a thriving trade developed.

The kingdoms of Ghana, Mali, and Songhay were in an excellent location to profit from the trade in gold and salt. Each of these kingdoms was located along the main trade routes in western Africa. The rulers of Ghana, Mali, and Songhay collected taxes on all goods that entered or left their kingdoms. As a result, they became very wealthy.

Through the years, large trading cities grew up in the grasslands of western Africa. Merchants came to these cities from hundreds of miles away to exchange their goods. In the center of each city was a large and busy marketplace where many different kinds of goods were on display. For example, there were ivory, ebony,* and honey from the forests of tropical Africa. From the lands to the north of the Sahara came such goods as wheat, horses, salt, dates, and cloth. Many people in Ghana, Mali, and Songhay earned their living from trade.

The kingdoms of Ghana, Mali, and Songhay all had strong, efficient governments. Each of the three kingdoms of western Africa was headed by a powerful ruler, who was treated with great honor. Thousands of people in each kingdom helped the ruler carry on the work of government. For example, in

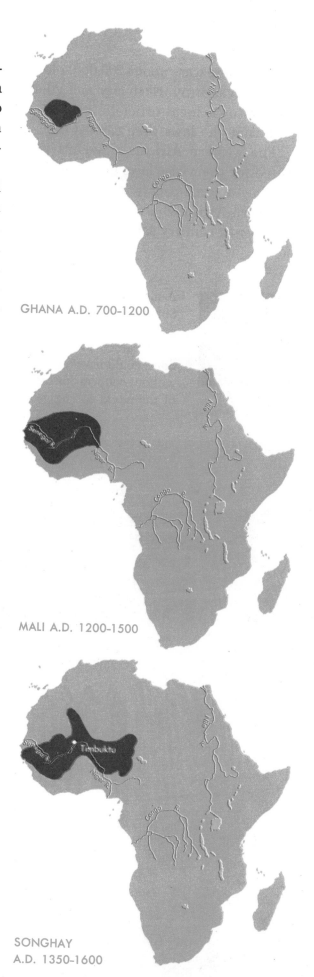

GHANA A.D. 700–1200

MALI A.D. 1200–1500

SONGHAY
A.D. 1350–1600

Three early African kingdoms. These kingdoms grew up in the western grasslands south of the Sahara. What facts about land, climate, and natural resources help explain why civilizations developed in this part of the continent?

39

Ghana there were about 200,000 soldiers in the royal army. Each city and village had its own local officials, who made sure that the laws were carried out.

The western African kingdoms were noted for their wise laws and their honest, law-abiding people. A traveler from northern Africa who visited Mali in the fourteenth century said that the people there loved justice and fair play more than any other people he had seen. This visitor also said that a person could travel throughout Mali in complete safety, without ever being robbed or harmed in any way. This respect for laws may help to explain why the kingdoms of western Africa became so powerful and prosperous.

Cooperation

See pages 178-181

A mosque in Songhay may have looked very much like this artist's drawing. Songhay, Ghana, and Mali were three powerful kingdoms that grew up in the grasslands of western Africa hundreds of years ago. Many people in these kingdoms earned their living from trade. Do you think the people of these kingdoms could have traded so successfully with people from other parts of Africa without cooperation? Do you think it would be possible for people in any part of the world to engage in trade without cooperation? Explain your answers.

Arab visitors from the north brought their form of writing and their religion to the people of the grassland kingdoms. In early times, the people who lived in the grasslands of western Africa did not have any form of writing. They communicated mainly by talking to one another. In about the eighth century, however, Arabs from northern Africa began coming to the grasslands. Most of the newcomers were traders. They brought with them the Arabic form of writing. Because of their learning and their skill as traders, some Arabs were employed as government officials by the rulers of the western African kingdoms.

The Arabs also brought the Islamic religion to western Africa. Many government officials and wealthy merchants in the western kingdoms became loyal followers of Islam. To show their loyalty, some of the rulers of the kingdoms of western Africa made the long and difficult journey to Mecca,* the holy city of Islam, in Arabia. They also spent large sums of money to build beautiful mosques where people could go to worship God.

In some of the larger cities of western Africa, there were Moslem* schools. A few of these schools were for older students, and somewhat resembled the universities of today. The most famous was the university at Timbuktu, in Songhay. Students came to Timbuktu from distant lands to study such subjects as law, religion, and medicine.

One by one, the great kingdoms of western Africa came to an end. For a time, each of the kingdoms that developed in the western African grasslands was rich and powerful. Ghana reached the height of its power about A.D. 1050. Mali's empire was especially strong and

prosperous about A.D. 1325, while Songhay reached its peak about two hundred years later.

As time passed, each of the great kingdoms of western Africa came to an end. Moslems from northern Africa began attacking Ghana in 1054, and in 1076 they captured the capital of the kingdom. The conquerors remained in Ghana for only a short while, but after they left, the kingdom never regained its power. In the early part of the thirteenth century, Ghana finally collapsed entirely.

Mali began to decline in the middle of the fourteenth century. Peoples living to the south and west attacked the outlying parts of the kingdom and weakened the control of the Mali rulers. Within the kingdom itself, members of the royal family quarreled over who was to be the next ruler. These quarrels probably made it even more difficult for the Mali rulers to hold the kingdom together. By the sixteenth century, most of Mali had been conquered by Songhay.

Quarrels over who was to rule also helped bring about the downfall of Songhay. These quarrels began in the early part of the sixteenth century and greatly weakened the government. In 1590, an army from Morocco invaded the weakened kingdom, and eventually many of Songhay's cities fell into ruin. By the beginning of the seventeenth century, the kingdom no longer existed.

Although the kingdoms of the grasslands all came to an end, they greatly influenced the later history of Africa. Stories about the great wealth of these kingdoms reached the people of Europe and made them eager to learn more about Africa. In Chapter 4, you will learn what happened when Europeans began visiting this continent.

The forest kingdoms of central Africa made use of many valuable resources. What were they?

Central Africa

Forest kingdoms grew up along the Gulf of Guinea. At about the same time people were settling in the grasslands south of the Sahara, other groups of people probably journeyed still farther south into the forest region along the Gulf of Guinea. (Compare the map on page 5 with the vegetation map on page 16.) The dense rainforests in this region protected them from more powerful groups of people and provided them with wood from which they made many useful articles. The hot, humid climate in that part of Africa was good for growing certain crops, such as yams and rice. As we have learned, the rainforests also had large deposits of gold, which the forest people traded for other goods with people who lived to the north.

Over the years, many different kingdoms grew up along the Gulf of Guinea. Among the best-known of these are Ife and Benin.* These kingdoms were established in the southern part of what is now Nigeria. The people who built these kingdoms were the ancestors of the Yoruba peoples who make their homes in that part of Africa today.

The kingdom of Ife may have begun about A.D. 1000. It probably reached the height of its power in the thirteenth century. By then, the people of Ife lived in great, walled cities. They were ruled by powerful kings and their courts.

By the thirteenth century, some of the people of Ife had become artists. They had learned how to make figures out of clay and bronze. Many of these beautiful figures were used in religious ceremonies. Others were used to decorate the royal courts of the Ife rulers.

The kingdom of Benin developed somewhat later than the kingdom of Ife. The capital of this kingdom, Benin City, was an important center for trade in western Africa for many centuries. The people of Benin used cowrie* shells and rings of metal for money. They traded weapons, farming tools, wood carvings, and food products for goods from other parts of Africa.

Some of the people of Benin were excellent artists. They may have learned how to make figures of brass* or bronze from their neighbors at Ife. Among the most famous works made by the people of Benin are the beautiful bronze plaques that once decorated the courtyard of the king's palace. These plaques tell the story of life in Benin for a period of about 140 years.

Migrations began in the rainforest of the Congo* River basin. Around the first century A.D., a series of great migrations had its beginnings in the forests of the

A plaque made by the artists of Benin. The kingdom of Benin was located in what is now southern Nigeria. Some of the people who lived in this kingdom were excellent artists. They made beautiful figures of brass or bronze. What does the plaque above tell you about the people of Benin and their way of life?

Congo River basin. People who had been living in what is now the country of Cameroon (see map on page 5) moved eastward and southward into other parts of the Congo basin. These people spoke a form of the Bantu language. Over the years, their descendants continued to migrate to different parts of southern and eastern Africa.

These early Bantu peoples probably left their homes north of the Congo River because of the rapid growth in their population. Even though they had learned how to make and use iron farming tools, they were eventually unable to produce enough food for all the people in their growing communities. As a result, different groups of Bantu peoples continued to travel into other parts of Africa in search of new land to farm.

Bantu kingdoms were established in several parts of the Congo River basin. Most of the Bantu peoples who settled in the Congo River basin probably lived in

Wood carvings. Long ago, people in the Bantu kingdoms of the Congo River basin carved beautiful objects out of wood. These objects greatly resembled the wooden articles made by African artists today. Some of these carvings, such as the one on the opposite page, were made to express religious feelings and beliefs. Artists also carved designs on useful objects, such as the cup at left, to express their feelings and their love of beauty. What are some other ways in which people express their feelings and thoughts? Do research in other sources about African sculpture and other arts to discover more about the ways in which African artists express themselves.

small communities with their own governments. As the years passed, some of these communities may have joined together under the rule of a single leader. By the fifteenth century, several well-organized Bantu kingdoms had developed. One of these was the kingdom of Kongo, which was located just south of the Congo River. This powerful kingdom had a prosperous capital city, a royal court, and an efficient system of collecting taxes.

Many people in the Bantu kingdoms of the Congo River basin became skilled craft workers. Some became excellent weavers. They made useful articles out of raffia, a fiber made from palm leaves. Bantu craft workers and artists also made beautiful objects out of wood. They probably carved spoons, masks, cups, and other objects. Artists in Africa today are famous for their wood carvings. These carvings greatly resemble articles made by their ancestors.

Eastern Africa

Trade grew up along Africa's east coast.
By the first century A.D., sailors from
Egypt and other lands along the Red
Sea (see map on page 5) were visiting
the east coast of Africa as far south as
what is now Tanzania. They traded with
the small groups of people living there.
In exchange for glassware, metal tools,
and cotton cloth, they received ivory
and other products.

About this same time, the Bantu peoples were beginning to migrate eastward.
By A.D. 400, some of them had probably
settled among the people living on the
east coast. Also by this time, other traders had begun to visit this part of Africa.
These merchant sailors came from
Southwest Asia, India, and other parts
of Asia. Many of the new traders were
Arabs.

By the tenth century, Arabs had
taken over much of the east coast trade.
Some of them settled in the coastal
towns and intermarried with the Bantu
people. Bantu customs and Arabic
customs became intermixed. The people came to speak a language called
Swahili, a mixture of Bantu and Arabic
languages. Because they spoke this
language, the people of the east coast
became known as the Swahili.

As the years passed, the villages and
towns along the east coast grew into
busy port cities, such as Kilwa, Mombasa, and Malindi. (See map on page
49.) Their merchant rulers were usually
followers of the Islamic faith, and
many large mosques were built in the
coastal towns.

The Swahili people also developed a
rich culture of their own. As early as
the twelfth century, Swahili poets were
writing beautiful songs in their own language. They continued to write songs
and poems for many centuries. Even today, modern African writers are famous
for their poems in Swahili.

Trade along the east coast continued to prosper for hundreds of years. Merchants from some of the port cities traveled inland to obtain gold, ivory, copper, and iron to sell to Asian traders.

The most prosperous of the east African ports was the island city of Kilwa, located off the coast of what is now the country of Tanzania. (See map on page 5.) In the early 1300's, a visitor to Kilwa

Ruins of the Great Mosque at Kilwa. The busy port city of Kilwa was the main trading center in eastern Africa for hundreds of years. Why do you suppose this was so? Why did people living in Kilwa build many large mosques? Do research in this chapter to discover why this city finally fell into ruins.

An Arab ship in the present-day harbor of Mombasa. Oceangoing ships similar to the one shown above were used hundreds of years ago by Arab traders who visited the eastern coast of Africa.

from the northern part of Africa described the city as "one of the most beautiful and well-constructed towns in the world." When Portuguese explorers stopped at Kilwa in 1500 (see map below), they were amazed at the fine houses made of coral.* They were also surprised at the wealth of the people. One of the early Portuguese visitors described the people as wearing clothing of "fine cotton and silk."

Kilwa established a mint which, at the height of the city's power, made coins of several different values. The city also demanded high taxes from the Arab and Indian traders who visited its port.

The east coast trade helped inland African kingdoms become prosperous. As the Arab and Indian traders continued to seek more and more goods from Africa's coastal cities, trade spread farther inland. Eventually, people from the inland kingdoms began to bring their goods to the markets of the coastal cities. Copper came from deposits worked by the Luba and Lunda peoples who lived west of Lake Tanganyika, in what is now the Republic of Zaire. Ivory, rhinoceros horn, and other goods were also carried to the coastal cities. In exchange, the inland people received such goods as cloth and pottery.

The inland kingdom that benefited most from the east coast trade was probably Monomotapa. (See map below.) This kingdom once covered a large area in southeastern Africa. In this part of the continent, there were many mineral deposits. The most important minerals were gold and iron ore. People

A Problem To Solve
The map at right shows the location of some of the early kingdoms and cities of eastern Africa. As you can see, three of these cities grew up along the coast. Why did these coastal cities grow and prosper for hundreds of years? In forming hypotheses to solve this problem, you will need to consider the following:
1. the location of these cities
2. the natural resources of eastern Africa
3. the sailing ability of ocean-going people from other lands

See Skills Manual, "Solving Problems"

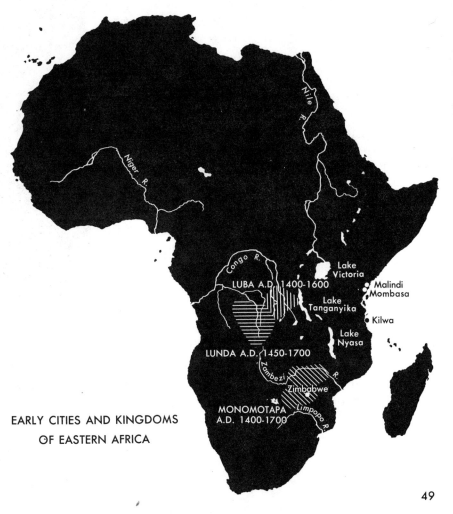

EARLY CITIES AND KINGDOMS
OF EASTERN AFRICA

49

here probably mined deposits of these minerals as early as the sixth century.

During the eleventh century, a group of Bantu people from the Luba area settled among the early people of Monomotapa. The newcomers soon became the ruling people in that area. They helped to increase trade with the people of the east coast. They even encouraged the Swahili merchants to visit their growing empire. The people of Monomotapa traded gold, iron, and ivory for the goods these merchants brought. As trade increased, the people of Monomotapa became more and more wealthy.

The capital of the Monomotapa kingdom was the great city of Zimbabwe.* (See map on page 49.) It was in this city that the king of Monomotapa lived. His stone palace was enclosed by an oval wall made of skillfully cut stone. In many places, this wall was thirty feet high and up to twenty feet thick.

Africa's eastern kingdoms lost their power. The cities along the east coast flourished for hundreds of years. But they lost their power soon after the coming of the Portuguese at the end of the fifteenth century. (See pages 55-56.) The Portuguese wanted to profit from the trade in gold and other goods. They attacked some of the prosperous port cities. From others they demanded huge tributes of gold and ivory. The Portuguese were armed with guns, and they attacked without warning. As a result, they were able to defeat or frighten away the city dwellers. By 1510, most of the east African port cities were under Portuguese control.

The kingdom of Monomotapa also lost much of its power about this time. Another African kingdom, called Changamire, grew up to the south. It

took over much of Monomotapa, including the city of Zimbabwe. Changamire remained strong for about three hundred years. Then, in the 1830's, it was destroyed by invaders from the south. The great city of Zimbabwe fell into ruins.

Migration

The ruins of Zimbabwe, an ancient city in southeastern Africa. These ruins are located in the present-day country of the same name. The city of Zimbabwe was once the capital of the Monomotapa kingdom. (See map on page 49.) This kingdom was ruled by Bantu people who settled there hundreds of years ago. Many other groups of Bantu people also migrated to new areas in southern and eastern Africa. What was the reason for this great migration?

4 Later History

Before 1400, Europeans knew little about Africa. The people who lived in Europe at the start of the 1400's knew very little about the great continent that lay to the south of them. For centuries, Europeans had been trading with people who lived along the Mediterranean coast of Africa. South of the coast, however, stretched the great Sahara. Few Europeans had ever crossed this hot, dry wasteland and returned to tell about their experiences.

Neither had Europeans sailed very far southward along the Atlantic coast of Africa. Sailors lacked accurate instruments for determining where they were if they lost sight of land. Also, their ships were small and unsafe, and could not sail very well against the wind. Near the African coast, the winds generally blow from north to south. Sailors were afraid that if they traveled too far southward, they would never be able to return home.

In the early 1400's, however, a few tiny ships began sailing farther and farther southward along Africa's west coast. These ships came from Portugal, a small country in southwestern Europe.

Why did the Portuguese want to sail southward along the African coast? There were several reasons why daring sailors from Portugal were willing to risk the dangers of sailing farther along the western coast of Africa. Let us see what some of those reasons were.

First, the Portuguese had heard exciting stories about the rich kingdoms south of the Sahara. (See pages 38-41.) Possibly they had seen some gold that came from these distant lands. They wanted to visit the African kingdoms, so they could get some of this gold for themselves.

Like most people in Europe, the Portuguese were Christians. For centuries, they had been fighting against the Moslems* who had invaded southern Europe. During this time, they had heard stories about a Christian king named Prester John. This man was said to rule over a great kingdom somewhere in Africa or Asia. Prester John was believed to be very rich and powerful. If the Portuguese could find him, he might help them in their wars against the Moslems.

There was another reason why the Portuguese wanted to sail along the coast of Africa. They wanted to find a sea route to the Indies.*

Many people in Europe bought spices, silks, and other valuable goods from the Indies. However, they had to pay very high prices for these items. The journey by land across the continent of Asia was long and difficult. Arab traders made this journey. They brought goods from the Indies to ports on the eastern shore of the Mediterranean Sea. There, traders from the Italian city of Venice loaded the goods on their ships and carried them to ports in Europe. The prices they charged for these goods were much higher than the prices the Arab traders paid in the Indies.

If the Portuguese could find an all-water route to the Indies, they could buy goods directly from merchants there. They would no longer have to pay high prices to Venetian traders.

Portuguese explorers sailed around the southern tip of Africa. In the early 1400's, several things happened that made it

*See Glossary

easier for sailors to go on long voyages. Instruments to help sailors find directions at sea were improved. Also, shipbuilders designed faster and safer vessels. These ships could sail more easily against the wind. The person who did the most to improve sailing methods was Prince Henry, a brother of Portugal's king. Prince Henry started a school where Portuguese sailors could learn new techniques of sailing. He also gave prizes and honors to sailors who journeyed farthest southward along the African coast.

Year after year, the search for an all-water route to the Indies continued. By 1446, Portuguese sailors had journeyed as far south as the Cape Verde Islands. (See map on page 55.) Later, other explorers reached the mouth of

Prince Henry of Portugal established a school for mariners and map makers in the early 1400's. What kinds of things did Portuguese sailors learn in this school? In what important way did Prince Henry hope these sailors would make use of the knowledge they gained in his school?

See pages 95-96

The Need for Faith

Vasco da Gama sailed around the Cape of Good Hope and discovered an all-water route to India. He and his crew suffered many hardships on their journey, yet da Gama would not turn back. Do you think da Gama could ever have made such a journey if he had not had faith in himself? Explain your answer. Do you think it is important for all explorers to have faith in themselves? Why? Why not? What other kinds of faith do you think explorers ought to have?

the Congo* River. In 1488, an explorer named Bartholomeu Dias rounded the southernmost tip of Africa.

An all-water route to the Indies was finally discovered by a Portuguese explorer named Vasco da Gama. In 1497, da Gama's four ships left the port of Lisbon and headed southward through the Atlantic Ocean. After many hardships, da Gama and his crew sailed around the Cape of Good Hope. (See map below.) Then they traveled up the eastern coast of Africa. Here they were surprised to find several rich cities that Arab traders had been visiting for centuries. (See pages 46-50). After sailing eastward across the Indian Ocean,

da Gama reached India in May, 1498. Several months later, he returned to Portugal with a cargo of spices and jewels.

The Portuguese built forts and trading posts along the African coast. In the years that followed da Gama's voyage, many Portuguese ships made the long journey around Africa to the Indies. They returned with cargoes of spices, jewels, and other valuable products. These were sold to people throughout Europe. Trade with the Indies brought great wealth to Portugal.

Not all the Portuguese who visited Africa were on their way to the Indies. Some Portuguese traders came to

The voyage of Vasco da Gama. Why were the Portuguese so eager to discover a new route to India? In what ways did da Gama's journey affect the European exploration and settlement of Africa?

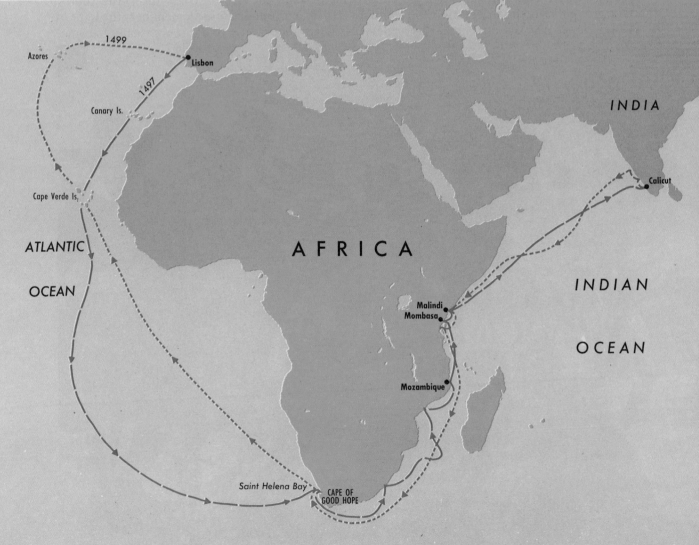

Africa to obtain goods which they could sell for high prices in Europe. These traders brought cloth, knives, jewelry, and other articles that Africans wanted. They exchanged these items for gold, ivory, and other products.

The Portuguese traders were sometimes attacked by Africans or by sailors from other European countries. To protect the traders, the Portuguese built a number of stone forts along the African coast. Some of these forts are still standing today.

Other Europeans began trading with the people of Africa. The Portuguese wanted to keep control of all trade with the lands they had discovered. However, they were not strong enough to prevent other European countries from sending expeditions to Africa and the Indies. One of these countries was Holland. In the 1600's, the Dutch* seized control of many Portuguese forts and trading posts in Africa. They also started new settlements along the African coast. In 1652, for example, a group of Dutch settlers founded a trading post near the Cape of Good Hope. Its purpose was to supply Dutch ships headed for the Indies. This settlement grew into an important city known as Cape Town.

Gradually, people from England, France, and other European countries also began coming to Africa. They, too, built forts and started trading with the people who lived there.

Dutch* traders and merchants established settlements along the African coast during the 1600's. One group of Dutch settlers landed in southern Africa and founded a settlement near the Cape of Good Hope. Why did they build this settlement? What important city did it eventually become?

For hundreds of years, Europeans who came to Africa seldom traveled far from the seacoast. On most of Africa's rivers, there were rapids that kept boats from sailing very far upstream. Dense forests, rugged mountains, and barren deserts made it hard to travel inland on foot or on horseback. Also, Europeans were not used to the hot, humid climate of central Africa. Many who came there died of tropical diseases such as malaria* and yellow* fever.

Because the dangers were so great, European merchants would not go to Africa unless they could be sure of making large profits. Two items were especially profitable for European traders. These were gold and slaves.

The African Slave Trade

In early times, slavery was common in many parts of the world. When Europeans began coming to Africa, most people did not think it was wrong for one human being to own another. Slavery had been practiced for thousands of years. For example, the Moslems in northern Africa often had Christian slaves. These were people who had been captured in battle or on ships at sea. The Christians, in turn, sometimes made slaves out of captured Moslems.

Slavery was also common among the peoples of central and southern Africa. Often, two neighboring ethnic* groups would go to war against each other. Enemy prisoners captured by each group were forced to become slaves. When European traders began visiting Africa, the people there were eager to buy cloth and other goods that the traders were selling. They were glad to trade some of their slaves to the Europeans in exchange for these goods.

Millions of Africans were taken to America as slaves. About 1500, something happened to make the slave trade much more profitable than it had been. Christopher Columbus and other explorers sailed westward across the Atlantic Ocean. They were searching for a new sea route to the Indies. Instead, they found the two great continents of North and South America. Soon other Europeans were sailing westward to establish colonies in these new lands.

Some of the Europeans who went to America started large farms called plantations. There they grew crops that could be sold for high prices in Europe. Many people were needed to work on these plantations. The colonists began to buy black slaves from Africa to do their work for them.

Between the early 1500's and the late 1800's, millions of black slaves were taken to North and South America. The African slave trade brought great suffering to these people. But it also had harmful effects on the people who stayed in Africa. The people of each ethnic group wanted to capture as many prisoners as possible to sell to the European traders. At the same time, they wanted to protect themselves from being sold into slavery. So wars between African groups took place more often and were fiercer than ever before.

Laws were passed to abolish slavery. During the 1700's, many people in Europe and America came to believe that slavery was wrong. Groups were formed to end the African slave trade. As time passed, one nation after another passed laws to end slavery. In the United

States, for example, slavery was abolished in 1865, after the Civil War.* The ending of slavery was an important step forward in human progress.

Africa Under European Rule

Europeans began to take a greater interest in Africa. As you have learned, people in Europe knew very little about the interior of Africa. Near the end of the 1700's, however, two daring explorers made journeys far inland. A Scotsman named James Bruce visited the remote country of Ethiopia. He discovered a lake that is one of the sources of the Nile River. Another Scotsman, Mungo Park, traveled much of the way along the Niger River. The exciting stories told by these explorers made Europeans eager to learn more about the great continent to the south.

There was another reason why Europeans became more interested in Africa. Fierce robbers, called the Barbary pirates, sailed from ports along Africa's northern coast. They attacked European and American trading ships in the Mediterranean Sea. The pirates robbed the ships of their valuable cargoes.

David Livingstone, a Scottish missionary, was one of the many Europeans who came to Africa in the nineteenth century. He explored much of central and southern Africa. (See map below.)

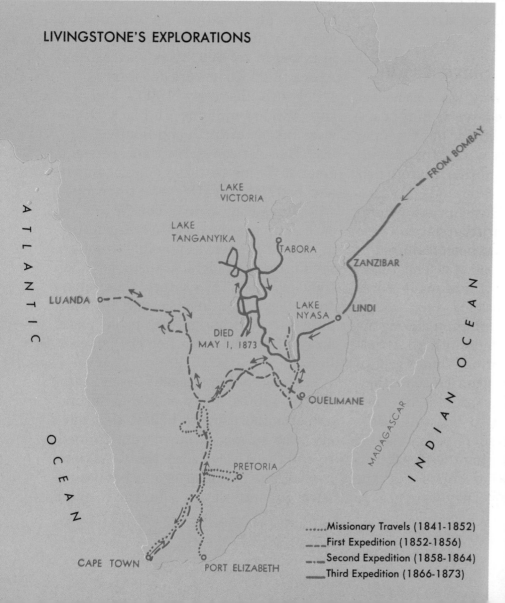

LIVINGSTONE'S EXPLORATIONS

......Missionary Travels (1841-1852)
--- First Expedition (1852-1856)
-·-·- Second Expedition (1858-1864)
___ Third Expedition (1866-1873)

They held the passengers and crews for ransom or sold them as slaves.

In the early 1800's, several European countries and the United States made a strong effort to get rid of the Barbary pirates. They sent naval fleets to destroy the pirate ships. They also attacked the hideouts of the pirates, which were along the African coast. In 1830, France sent troops into what is now Algeria. Within a few years, much of Algeria had been brought under French rule. And the Barbary pirates were no longer a threat to ships in the Mediterranean Sea.

Explorers, missionaries, and traders came to Africa from Europe. During the nineteenth century, many Europeans visited Africa or came there to live. Some of these people were explorers. They had a strong sense of curiosity and a love of adventure. These people faced many dangers in order to visit lands that no European had ever seen before. For example, David Livingstone explored much of central and southern Africa. (See map on opposite page.) While exploring along the Zambezi River, Livingstone reached a great waterfall. He named it Victoria Falls.

Henry M. Stanley and David Livingstone meet at Lake Tanganyika. Stanley was sent to Africa by an American newspaper to search for Livingstone, when people feared this great explorer was lost.

Another explorer, Henry M. Stanley, became the first European to travel all the way down the Congo River.

A number of Europeans who came to Africa in the nineteenth century were Christian missionaries.* At that time, many people in Africa worshiped gods that were not familiar to the Europeans. The missionaries wanted to convert the Africans to Christianity. They were sent to Africa by religious groups who provided the money needed to start missions in the wilderness.

The missionaries also came to Africa because they wanted to help the people there. During the nineteenth century, people in Europe were very proud of their achievements in such fields as science, industry, and education. They felt that Africans were "backward" and "uncivilized." This was because African ways of life were so different from their own. Many Europeans felt they had a "Christian duty" to help Africans learn to live as <u>they</u> did. They wanted to teach Africans how to read and write. They also wanted to heal people who were sick. To accomplish these goals, the missionaries built schools and hospitals in Africa.

Another group of people who came to Africa were traders. In the late 1700's, the Industrial Revolution had begun to take place in Europe. (See page 146.) Many new factories were built in Europe to produce manufactured goods. Factory owners began to realize that certain raw* materials found in Africa could be very useful in industry. Among these products were palm* oil, peanuts, cacao,* rubber, ivory, mahogany, and ebony.

In the 1800's, many European companies sent traders to Africa. These

people obtained raw materials from the Africans in return for cloth, guns, and other manufactured products. Often, daring traders journeyed far into the interior to exchange their goods.

European nations competed with each other to gain territories in Africa. In the last half of the nineteenth century, European countries began to take control of large territories in Africa. Among these countries were Great Britain, France, and Germany. They established colonies and sent government officials to rule over the Africans.

Several facts help to explain why European nations wanted to have colonies

Drying cacao beans in Ghana. Cacao, which is used in making chocolate, has long been an important crop in Africa. During the 1800's, several European nations wanted to obtain cacao and other raw materials for their factories. Partly for this reason, they established colonies in Africa. What other facts help explain why European nations wanted colonies on this continent?

in Africa. As you have learned, the European nations wanted to get raw materials from this continent. They also wanted to sell manufactured goods to the African people. They believed they could do this more easily if they ruled over territories in Africa. If they controlled Africa, they could start mines and plantations to produce the raw materials they needed. They could also build roads and railroads to transport these materials to seaports.

During the 1800's, many people believed a country could become rich by owning colonies in foreign lands. So European leaders found they could become more popular with their people by taking over territories in Africa.

Some European nations were not really eager to establish colonies in Africa. But they did so anyway. They feared that other nations might gain control of these territories and prevent them from trading. For example,

Great Britain took control of certain lands to keep them from being seized by the Germans or the French.

There were other reasons why Europeans wanted to rule over lands in Africa. They felt they were more "civilized" than the Africans. If they ruled over these people, they could bring them the benefits of European civilization. Also, the slave trade had not yet been ended completely in Africa. Some Europeans thought that by establishing colonies in Africa they could protect people there from slavery.

How the European nations gained control of African territories. As time passed, European countries took over more and more land in Africa. Sometimes they did this by signing treaties with the rulers of different ethnic groups. A European nation would agree to protect a certain group from its enemies. In return, the ruler of the group would promise to be loyal to the European country's government. Gradually African leaders were replaced with European officials, and a colony was established. Often the Europeans could persuade African rulers to obey them because they could supply manufactured goods the Africans wanted.

Many people in Africa did not want to be ruled by Europeans, however. Sometimes they went to war to keep the Europeans from taking over their land. But the European governments were much stronger and better organized than the African governments. The European soldiers were well trained, and they had more modern weapons. So they were able to win most of the battles they fought against the Africans.

By 1914, nearly all of Africa was ruled by European countries. (See map on page 66.) Great Britain, Germany, France, Belgium, Spain, Portugal, and Italy all had colonies on this continent. The only independent countries in Africa were Liberia and Ethiopia.

The Struggle for Independence

Many Africans were unhappy under colonial rule. After years of living under European rule, the native people of Africa became more and more dissatisfied. They had many complaints against the European settlers and government officials.

In some parts of Africa, for example, the Europeans took over the best farmland. They started plantations

Mining gold in the Republic of South Africa. During the time when much of Africa was under colonial rule, the Europeans established many mines. Some of these mines are still in operation today.

where rubber, cacao, and other crops were grown for export.* The native Africans could no longer use these lands for hunting and grazing. As a result, they were forced to move their families to poorer lands. Or they had to work for the Europeans at very low wages.

Many Africans refused to become hired laborers for the Europeans. But the Europeans needed many low-paid

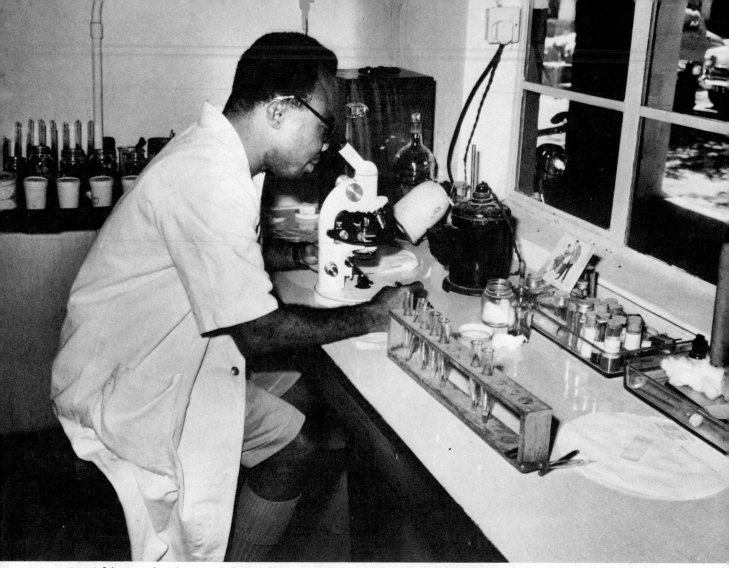

An African scientist at work. In the past, Europeans held most of the jobs in business and industry in Africa. Today many of these jobs are held by native Africans. What brought about this change?

workers so they could run their mines and plantations at a profit. To force the Africans to take jobs, the European governments began to tax them. This was a great hardship to many of the Africans, because they usually had no money. The only way they could get money was by working for the Europeans. Often the African workers earned little more than they needed to pay their taxes. There was seldom enough left over to buy food and clothing for their families. So the Africans remained poor, while most Europeans lived comfortably.

Under colonial rule, the native Africans had no voice in their own government. They were not allowed to vote. So there was little they could do to change the laws or to avoid the taxes that kept them poor.

Education caused more discontent. As you have learned, European missionaries started a number of schools in Africa. In these schools, African students learned about Western* ideas of freedom and democracy. They began to wonder why the Europeans did not follow these ideas in their treatment of the Africans.

Some students also learned that if they had enough education, they might get well-paying jobs. They began to dream of a better way of life. Many of them moved from the countryside to Africa's growing cities. There, some were able to get jobs as clerks, messengers, or servants. But they were still dissatisfied. They wanted to have the same things the Europeans enjoyed. However, many Europeans felt that nonwhite people were not capable of doing important work. They refused to hire native Africans for responsible, well-paying jobs. Many educated native Africans came to feel that there was only one way to get the things they wanted. This was by gaining complete freedom from European rule.

Africans began working together to reach their goals. The people who moved to Africa's cities often found life to be confusing and even frightening. In rural areas, the people of each ethnic group lived together in their own communities. People who belonged to the same group took care of one another. In the cities, however, life was very different. People in the cities came from many different ethnic groups. They were strangers to one another. So they did not take care of people who were ill or out of work, as they would have done at home.

Gradually, the newcomers to the cities came to know one another. They began meeting together to discuss their needs and problems. They found that by forming associations and cooperating with each other, they could begin to solve their problems.

The new associations helped in another way. In the past, the only groups that most Africans had ever belonged to were their ethnic groups. They had no feeling of loyalty toward a nation. But the new associations were made up of people from many different ethnic groups. As time passed, people began to feel a loyalty toward their new associations. This loyalty grew into a feeling of nationalism.*

World War II* strengthened the movement for independence. Although they longed for freedom, many Africans feared they would never gain it. They believed that their European rulers were so powerful they could never be defeated. In 1939, however, World War II began. During this war, many Africans served in British or French armies. Sometimes they saw the soldiers of the nation that ruled them beaten in battle. The Africans began to realize that their European masters were not as powerful as they had thought. This gave them hope that the Europeans might someday be forced to leave Africa.

Even the Africans who stayed at home were affected by World War II. The Allied* armies needed many goods that could be produced from African raw materials. Roads, railroads, and harbors were improved to make sure that these badly needed raw materials could be sent abroad. Workers in African mines and plantations earned more money than ever before. However, they could not buy the manufactured goods they wanted. Because of the war, these goods were no longer being shipped from Europe. This made the Africans unhappy, and they blamed the Europeans for the lack of goods.

Because Africa was so important to the war effort, other nations of the world became interested in African

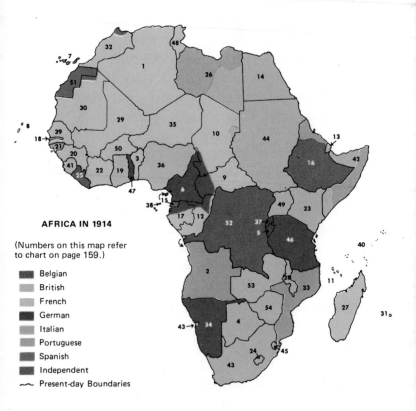

AFRICA IN 1914

(Numbers on this map refer to chart on page 159.)

- ■ Belgian
- ■ British
- ■ French
- ■ German
- ■ Italian
- ■ Portuguese
- ■ Spanish
- ■ Independent
- ⌒ Present-day Boundaries

In 1914, Ethiopia and Liberia were the only two independent countries in Africa. The rest of the African continent was divided up into colonies that were under European control.

problems. Among these countries were the United States and the Soviet Union. They criticized the European powers for the way they treated the Africans. The Americans told the European powers that they should let the people of Africa have a voice in their government.

Many African nations won their freedom from European rule. After World War II ended in 1945, African demands for independence became much stronger. The African people were tired of living in poverty. They wanted higher wages and lower taxes. They also wanted new roads, better health care, and free education. However, the European nations had been greatly weakened by the war. They did not have the huge

sums of money needed to build all the roads, schools, and hospitals that Africa lacked.

Meanwhile, Britain was making plans to free some of its colonies in Asia, such as India and Burma. Many Africans had fought in Asia during the war. They felt they had as much right to govern themselves as the Asians did. People in Africa began to organize groups to work for independence.

To prevent more unrest, Britain and France began giving Africans a larger voice in government. Africans were allowed to elect some of the members of the colonial lawmaking bodies. Also, a growing number of Africans were appointed to government jobs. But these reforms did not satisfy the Africans.

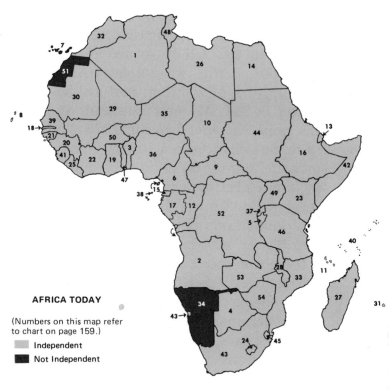

AFRICA TODAY

(Numbers on this map refer to chart on page 159.)

Independent

Not Independent

Today, there are more than fifty independent nations in Africa. One of these is Ghana, which won its freedom in 1957. The picture above shows a parade to celebrate Ghana's independence.

They wanted to be completely free of European rule.

As time passed, Africans began to show their discontent in more violent ways. In 1948, rioting and looting broke out in the British colony called the Gold Coast—now known as Ghana. Later, African rebels in Kenya began to attack farms and homes belonging to European settlers. Rebellions also broke out in Algeria and Morocco, two French colonies in northern Africa. The European powers knew it would take thousands of soldiers and huge sums of money to put down these uprisings. They no longer had the money and the military power to be successful. So they were forced to give the African colonies their freedom.

Starting in 1956, Britain and France granted independence to some of their colonies in Africa. But Algeria had to fight a long, bitter war to win its independence from France. Meanwhile, the Belgian Congo—now known as Zaire—gained its freedom from Belgium.

Angola, Mozambique, and Rhodesia* won their fight for independence. By the late 1960's, all the larger nations in northern and central Africa were free of foreign rule. In southern Africa, however, three large colonies were still ruled by Europeans. These three were Angola, Mozambique, and Rhodesia.

Angola and Mozambique were colonies of Portugal. This small country had been the first to start settlements in Africa. (See pages 55-56.) The

Portuguese did not want to give up their African possessions. However, they had treated the native Africans poorly. In the 1960's armed revolts broke out in the two colonies. After several years of fighting, Portugal admitted defeat. Mozambique and Angola gained independence in 1975.

Rhodesia had been a British colony since the late 1800's. Its government was controlled by white settlers.These people made up less than 4 percent of the population. Nearly all the rest were blacks, who had very little voice in the government. In 1965, the white settlers declared Rhodesia to be an independent country. They set up a new government run entirely by the whites. Britain, the United States, and other nations refused to recognize Rhodesia's independence.

In the early 1970's, black rebels in Rhodesia began fighting to overthrow the white government. After several years of conflict, the white leaders agreed to give up their power. Free elections were held' in 1980. A new government made up largely of blacks came to power. Soon afterward, Rhodesia became an independent nation called Zimbabwe.* Today there are more than fifty independent nations in Africa.(Compare maps on pages 66 and 67.)

The Struggle for Freedom Today

The struggle for freedom continues. Another country that has been torn by conflict between whites and nonwhites is the Republic of South Africa. Like Rhodesia, South Africa was a British colony.It became independent in 1931. At that time, the government of South Africa was controlled entirely by the white people who lived there. They were descendants of Dutch and British settlers who had come here many years earlier.(See pages 56-57.)

Today the white people continue to run South Africa's government, even though they make up only about 15 percent of the population. They also own most of the country's land and natural resources. The rest of the people, who are not white, have very few rights.

To keep its power over the nonwhite people, the South African government set up a system called apartheid.* Under apartheid, white people live completely apart from nonwhites.

The people who are considered to be nonwhite are divided into three groups. The largest group is the blacks. Their ancestors lived here in the earliest times. The blacks make up about 73 percent of South Africa's population. The other two groups are the Colored* and the Asians.* They make up about 12 percent of the population. Of these three groups the blacks have the fewest rights.

Many blacks live in "homelands." Ten areas of South Africa have been set aside as tribal homelands for blacks. Many of them live in these homelands today. The South African government wants these homelands to become independent nations where all blacks will live eventually. Four of the homelands have been declared independent by the government. But other nations have not accepted this claim. They say the homelands are merely a trick of the white South Africans to avoid sharing their power. Also, they point out that these homelands are all in areas with poor soil and few minerals.

Any blacks who are now living in a homeland must have permits to go outside the area. They must also carry passes to show who they are and where they live.

Many blacks live near large cities. There are millions of blacks who do not live in homelands. Most of these people live in communities outside of large cities such as Johannesburg. (See page 101.) Many of these "urban" blacks work in the city near where they live. They are not allowed to move freely about the city but must return to their community as soon as they leave work. They must also carry identification passes.

A fight against apartheid. Many people in South Africa who have spoken out against apartheid have been arrested and thrown into prison without a trial. There, some have been beaten or killed.

In recent years, the nonwhite people of South Africa have been growing more and more dissatisfied with their way of life. Many of them have been taking part in strikes, marches, and other demonstrations to protest apartheid. Some of these demonstrations have been peaceful. Others, however, have led to bloodshed. Hundreds of people have been killed or wounded, and much property destroyed.

Black people in Soweto, near Johannesburg, South Africa. More than one million blacks live in Soweto. In South Africa, under a system called apartheid, nonwhites live completely apart from whites.

Bishop Desmond Tutu. The picture above shows Tutu trying to convince a gathering of blacks not to use violence in their struggle against apartheid. One of South Africa's main leaders in the fight against apartheid, Tutu was awarded the Nobel Peace Prize* in 1984. What is apartheid? Why was Tutu awarded the Nobel Prize? What are some nonviolent ways people in Africa and other parts of the world are fighting against apartheid? Do research to find answers to these questions.

Many white people in South Africa feel that apartheid should come to an end. For example, in the summer of 1985, ninety-one of South Africa's leading white business people ran full page newspaper advertisements calling for an end to apartheid.

People all over the world are deeply concerned about the treatment of non-whites in South Africa. The South Af-rican government has been criticized strongly by the United Nations and other world organizations. Some countries have stopped trading with South Africa. Others are refusing to give financial aid. France withdrew its ambassador. Many people in the United States have demanded their city or state governments stop doing business with companies that have operations in South Africa.

These pressures at home and from countries throughout the world, along with strikes, riots, and bloodshed have had an effect on the South African government. They are finding out that apartheid does not work.In early 1986 they plan to vote on doing away with the passes that nonwhites have been required to carry. Many people think that this is an important step.But they also say that the violence in South Africa will continue until apartheid ends and <u>all</u> the people here have equal rights.

Namibia* faces an uncertain future. The unrest in South Africa has spread to the neighboring territory of Namibia. (See map on page 5.) This territory has been governed by South Africa since World War I.* Blacks make up more than 85 percent of the population in Namibia while whites make up only 7½ percent. As in South Africa, the government keeps its power over the blacks by using the system of apartheid.

In recent years, there has been fighting between South African troops and Namibian blacks who want their country to be independent. Also, the United Nations and many countries throughout the world are working to gain independence for Namibia.

Some democratic and Communist* nations have sent aid to Africa. In recent years an important rivalry has been taking place in Africa. The rivals are two groups of nations located in other parts of the world. On one side are democratic Western* nations such as the United States, Britain, and France. On the other side are Communist nations such as the Soviet Union, East Germany, and Cuba.

The Western nations would like to see democratic governments established throughout Africa. They would also like to carry on trade with the African countries. To achieve these goals the Western nations have helped African countries in a number of ways.For example, they have given them money as well as food and other supplies. They have also sent advisors to help them solve their economic* problems.

The Communist nations would like the African countries to adopt communism as a way of life. So they, too, have been sending money,supplies,and advisors to nations in Africa. Sometimes they have also sent troops and weapons to support governments that seem friendly toward communism.

Two countries that have received large amounts of military aid from the Communists are Angola and Ethiopia. The present government of Angola came to power with the help of weapons and other military supplies from the Soviet Union. In addition, Cuba sent about 20,000 soldiers to Angola. Many of these troops are still stationed in this country. The Soviet Union and Cuba also sent help to the government of Ethiopia when it was trying to put down a revolt by some of its people.(See page 78.) Today, Ethiopia is closely allied with the Communist nations.

Africa Today

The young nations of Africa face many problems. Independence has not solved all of the problems facing the people of Africa. Many of the African countries have had great difficulty setting up stable governments. Often there are not enough well-trained people to carry on the work of government. Also, millions of Africans lack a feeling of loyalty toward their nations. In Chapter 5, you can read more about the problems of government in Africa.

The African countries also suffer from other serious problems today. Most of these countries are still very poor, and there are not enough jobs for everyone. It is hard for most people to get a good education. In re-

Mothers preparing a school lunch in Burkina Faso. Large numbers of people in Africa do not get enough food to eat. As a result, millions have died of hunger and disease. Do you think a school lunch program is a good way of helping to solve this problem? Explain your answer.

Delegates from Nigeria at the General Assembly of the United Nations in New York City. Today the African countries play a very important part in this world organization. Why is this so?

cent years, some African countries have not been able to produce enough food for their people. As a result, millions of Africans have died of hunger or disease. Chapter 13 tells more about the problems facing Africa's developing nations.

Africans are working together to achieve progress. Although the people of Africa face serious problems, they are proud of their independence. They are trying to establish the kinds of government that will best meet their needs. And they are working hard to improve their way of life. (See Chapter 13.)

To reach these goals, Africa's people are cooperating through the Organization of African Unity. The OAU was established in 1963. Nearly all of the independent African countries are now members. One of the major duties of the OAU is to keep peace between member nations. This organization has helped to settle several border disputes. In addition, the OAU is working to improve relations between different ethnic groups in Africa.

The OAU has given the African people an important voice in world affairs. All of its members belong to the United Nations. They often consult together before voting on important issues before the UN. Members of the OAU make up nearly one third of the UN's total membership. So they have great influence in this organization when they act together.

Rules and Government

See pages 178-181

Campaigning before elections in Senegal. When the African nations gained independence from colonial rule, most of their citizens had never taken part in government. As a result, self-government has been difficult for many African nations. Discuss the following questions about government with your classmates.

1. What are some of the responsibilities citizens have toward their government?
2. In what ways do citizens learn how to fulfill these responsibilities?
3. What has made it difficult for many African people to take part in their governments?

5 Government

The countries of Africa are governed in many different ways. On the continent of Africa today, there are more than fifty independent countries. The people of each country have their own history and their own way of life. So it is not surprising that each country also has its own form of government.

Most of the countries in Africa today call themselves republics.* A few countries are monarchies.* In each of these, a king or queen is the official head of the government. Often, however, this person has little real power.

Some African countries have governments that are quite democratic. In a few African nations today, the people have a large share in the government. Free elections are held at regular times. In these elections, citizens can choose the people they want to make and carry out the laws. There is more than one political party, so voters have a choice of candidates. In these countries, people enjoy a great deal of freedom. They can criticize their leaders and try to make changes in the government. Nations that have governments like these are known as democracies.

Most African countries do not have truly democratic governments. In most Afri-

*See Glossary

can countries, the government is run by a single leader or a small group of leaders. Often these people allow little or no opposition to their rule. Elections are sometimes held in these countries. However, the people in power often find ways to keep other leaders from running against them. Usually only one political party is allowed by law. There is less freedom than there is in democracies. People who speak out against the government may be put in jail. Newspapers are allowed to print only what the government leaders want people to know.

In some countries, there are frequent changes in government. The governments of African countries do not always stay in power for very long. Sometimes a military leader will seize control of a nation's government by force. This leader will rule as a dictator* until his methods arouse strong opposition. Then other leaders will overthrow the dictator and set up a new government.

Sometimes the national government cannot keep order in a country. This may happen because the leaders are doing a poor job, or because different groups are struggling for power. The leaders of a country's armed forces may decide it is their duty to solve this problem. They will take over the government and rule until order has been restored. Then they will turn over their power to civilian leaders.

Problems of Government

Why have African countries found it so hard to establish long-lasting, democratic governments? To answer this question, you need to know something about Africa's history.

Few African countries were fully prepared for self-government. In Chapter 4, you discovered how the African nations won their freedom from European rule. Most Africans were eager for the chance to govern themselves. However, few countries in Africa were prepared

Students at the National School of Administration, in Niger. This west African country gained its independence from France in 1960 and set up a school to train students for jobs in its new government.

for self-government when the day of independence finally came.

In the early years of colonial rule, Africans had not been allowed to hold positions of leadership. Gradually, Britain and France began training some Africans to hold jobs in the government. But far too few Africans were prepared to take over the work that had been done for so long by Europeans. When independence came, most countries did not have enough well-trained people to run the government.

During the colonial period, few Africans had a chance to go to school. Of these few, only a handful went on to colleges and universities. As a result, most people in the new nations of Africa could not read and write. Without these skills, it was hard for them to be responsible citizens. They could not get all the information they needed to make wise decisions about government.

Today this situation is slowly changing. More Africans are learning to read and write. Also, more people have been trained to hold jobs in government. However, most African countries still do not have enough well-educated citizens.

Many Africans lack a feeling of loyalty to a national government. Another serious problem has made it difficult for African nations to establish strong, democratic governments. This problem is the lack of unity among the people of each nation.

Since early times, there have been hundreds of different ethnic* groups in Africa. (See page 84.) The people of each group have their own language and share the same ways of living and working. They usually feel a special loyalty toward members of their own group. Often they dislike or distrust the people of other groups.

As you know, several European countries divided Africa among themselves in the 1800's. The Europeans did not care how the new boundaries affected the different groups of people living in Africa. Most of the European colonies included several ethnic groups within their borders. Often the boundary lines divided the territory in which a large group lived. As a result, some members of the group lived in one colony and some in another. It is not surprising that the different groups in each colony did not feel they belonged together. Usually, these groups felt no loyalty toward their colonial governments.

During the fight for independence, the ethnic groups in each colony usually worked together. This was because they all shared the common goal of freedom. Since independence, however, many ethnic groups have had trouble cooperating with one another. Most Africans are still used to thinking of themselves as members of an ethnic group rather than as citizens of a country. They generally vote for leaders who belong to their own group. In this way, they try to make sure that their group has its fair share of power in the country.

Fighting has sometimes broken out between different ethnic groups. In some African nations, the rivalry between ethnic groups has led to tragic civil* wars. One example is Nigeria, the African country with the largest population. There are more than 250 different ethnic groups in Nigeria. In 1967, some of these groups tried to break away from Nigeria and form a separate country, called Biafra. It took the national government about two and one-half years to put down this uprising. Thousands of people were killed in the fighting or died of hunger and disease.

Trouble also arose in the easternmost part of the continent. This area is sometimes called the "Horn of Africa." In the country of Somalia, nearly all the people belong to an ethnic group called the Somalis. There are also Somalis in the neighboring countries of Ethiopia, Kenya, and Djibouti. Government leaders in Somalia would like to unite all the areas occupied by Somalis into a single nation. In 1977, some of the Somalis in eastern Ethiopia revolted against the national government there. Somalia sent troops to help the rebels. As a result, a war broke out between Ethiopia and Somalia. Ethiopia, with the help of the Soviet Union and Cuba, won this war in 1978. But there is still much unrest among Somali people who live in eastern Ethiopia.

In recent years, several other African nations have been torn by civil wars between different ethnic groups. Among these countries are Chad, Angola, Uganda, and Mozambique.

Some African leaders have a distrust of democracy. There is still another reason why it has been hard to establish democratic governments in Africa. The leaders of some African countries lack faith in democracy. They feel that it cannot work in countries where most of the people are poor and uneducated. These leaders claim that they should have the power to rule just as they please. Only then, they say, can they do whatever is necessary to help their countries make progress.

Some African leaders have been attracted by Communist* teachings. Often these people have been influenced by propaganda* from Communist nations such as the Soviet Union. The Communists blame the United States and the democratic nations of western Europe for most of Africa's problems. They also claim that communism is the best form of government for developing nations like those in Africa. Today several African countries, such as Ethiopia and Angola, have governments based on Communist ideas. These governments do not allow any real opposition.

African governments have often been unable to keep their promises to the people. The early years of independence were a time of great hope in Africa. Most Africans expected that independence would lead to great improvements in their way of life. Some people hoped to own their own farmland. Others hoped for more schools, better housing, and better jobs.

In some African countries, however, independence brought great disappointment. To win their people's support in the fight for independence, some leaders made promises they could not possibly keep. Others used their new positions only to help themselves become rich. As time passed, people discovered that many needed improvements were not being made. They also learned that some of their leaders were spending large amounts of money on themselves. As a result, the people became deeply dissatisfied. In a number of African countries, the discontent led to riots and other acts of violence. This made it easier for military leaders to take over the government.

Loyalty

See pages 178-181

People in Lagos, Nigeria. During the late 1960's, this country was the scene of a bitter civil war. Several other African countries have also been torn by fighting between different groups of people. Why has there been such a lack of unity among the people of each nation? What do you think might be done to solve this problem? Do you think it is important for people to have a strong feeling of loyalty toward their nation? Explain your answer.

The legislature* of Cameroon is called the National Assembly. Its members are elected by the people of Cameroon. Is it important for the members of the Assembly to place loyalty to their country before loyalty to their own ethnic group? Why do you think this?

A struggle for survival. Today, like other newly independent countries before them, the young nations of Africa are struggling for survival. They are faced with many problems. To help solve these problems, the people in individual countries must put loyalty to their national government before loyalty to their own ethnic group. Also it is necessary for the African nations to work more closely together. You can learn more about Africa's problems and what is being done to help solve them in Chapter 13.

Investigate Ancient African Civilizations

Three great civilizations that developed in Africa long ago were those of Egypt, the kingdom of Kush, and the kingdom of Mali. To discover more about these civilizations, you may wish to do the following:

1. As a class, make a study of the ancient Egyptian civilization. First, divide the class into committees. Then have each committee select one or two of the following topics for special study.

   a. farming   f. language
   b. arts   g. government
   c. religion   h. science
   d. cities   i. education
   e. trade   j. architecture

   Members of each group should make a plan for doing research and decide how to present the understandings they gain. In addition to preparing oral or written reports, consider presenting information in ways such as:

   a. murals (such as a mural showing people working at different crafts)
   b. skits (such as a short play illustrating the religious beliefs of the people)
   c. models and dioramas (such as a model of a pyramid)

2. On your own, do research and prepare a written report about the kingdom of Kush or the kingdom of Mali. In your report, you may wish to include information such as:
   a. location of the kingdom
   b. when the kingdom was at its height
   c. famous rulers and their accomplishments
   d. important cities   f. trade
   e. religion   g. education

Be a Biographer

Several of the people who led the struggles for independence in Africa later became government leaders in their newly independent nations. Choose one of the leaders listed below and do research about him.

Jomo Kenyatta   Kenneth Kaunda
Julius Nyerere   Mobutu Sese Seko
Habib Bourguiba   (See Mobutu)

Write a biography about this person and share your discoveries with other members of your class. In your biography, you may wish to include information such as the following:
1. this person's accomplishments
2. where and when he was born
3. where he was educated

Refer to pages 4-5 of the Skills Manual for help in finding information.

Thinking Together

Beginning in the late 1800's, the African people grew more and more dissatisfied under the rule of the Europeans. What caused their growing discontent? Discuss this question as a class. To prepare for your discussion, you will need to consider the ways in which the Africans were affected by the following:

1. education
2. way of life of the Europeans living in Africa
3. migration to the cities
4. associations formed in the cities
5. World War II

Chapter 4 of this book contains much information that will help you solve this problem. You may also wish to do research in other sources.

Explore Government in Africa

Since gaining independence from European rule, many African countries have had difficulty in establishing and maintaining stable governments. For example, since the early 1960's, more than seventy African leaders have been overthrown. Is it important for a country to have a stable government? Discuss this question as a class. To prepare for your discussion, the class should divide into committees. Each committee should choose a different African country and do research in other sources about the history of that country's government. The Skills Manual provides suggestions that will help you to locate and evaluate information and to hold a successful discussion.

Part 3
People and Their Way of Life

If you were to take a trip through Africa, you would find that many different peoples make their homes on this vast continent. What would you like to discover about the peoples of Africa? Make a list of the questions you would like to answer as you do research in Part 3 of this book. Your list might include questions such as the following.

- What are some of the different groups of people who live in Africa?
- What is life like in an African village?
- What types of houses do African villagers live in?
- What are some of Africa's largest cities? Which ones would you particularly like to visit?
- In what ways is life in an African city similar to city life in our country? In what ways is it different?
- What types of clothing do the different African peoples wear?
- In what ways is education in Africa similar to education in our country? In what ways is it different?

An open-air market in Ivory Coast. Many African cities have colorful markets where food products and many other goods are sold.

6 People

If we wanted to meet all of Africa's different peoples, we would have to travel for many months. Africa is a huge continent with a population of about 550 million.

The map on the opposite page shows that Africa as a whole is very thinly populated. The most crowded part of the continent is the Nile Delta.* The Nile River provides water for irrigating farmlands. For this reason, Egypt is often called "the gift of the Nile." Other densely populated areas are in parts of the continent where there is much farming, mining, or industry.

There are hundreds of different ethnic* groups in Africa. Most Africans are descended from Negroid* people who were living on this continent thousands of years ago. (See Chapter 3.) Some are descendants of Arabs* and Jews* who came from Southwest Asia during the last fifteen hundred years. A much smaller number of people are of European or Asian descent. (See pages 93-94.)

For centuries, people of these different ethnic groups have intermarried. Therefore, many Africans today are a mixture of different peoples. They

*See Glossary

People, in Tanzania. Hundreds of different peoples live in Africa. For example, in Tanzania there are more than 130 different ethnic groups. Each of these ethnic groups has its own language.

vary in skin color from light tan to dark brown.

More than one thousand different languages are spoken on the continent of Africa. Usually each ethnic group has its own language. In countries where there are many different ethnic groups, people often have great difficulty communicating with one another. To help overcome the language barrier, many people speak a European language such as English or French. These languages were brought to Africa during the time of colonial rule. Often, a European language is the official language of a country. For example, English is the official language of Nigeria, and French is the official

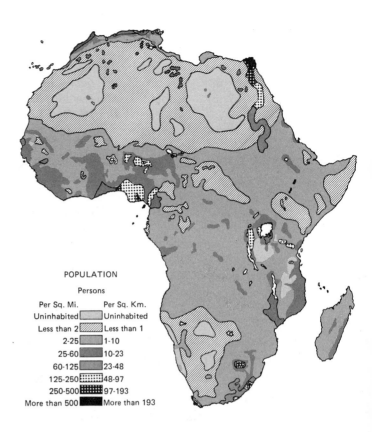

POPULATION

Persons

Per Sq. Mi.		Per Sq. Km.
Uninhabited		Uninhabited
Less than 2		Less than 1
2-25		1-10
25-60		10-23
60-125		23-48
125-250		48-97
250-500		97-193
More than 500		More than 193

A Problem To Solve
Africa is a huge continent with a population of about 550 million. However, as the map above shows, many of Africa's people live in a few densely populated areas. Why is the rest of the continent of Africa so thinly populated? To solve this problem, you will need to make several hypotheses. In forming your hypotheses, you will need to consider facts about the following in Africa:
1. land features and climate
2. ways of earning a living
3. location of natural resources
4. types and location of industry
5. transportation
Other chapters of this book also contain information that will be helpful in solving this problem. Refer to pages 4-5 of the Skills Manual for suggestions on finding information in other sources.

See Skills Manual, "Solving Problems"

Meeting
Needs

See pages 95-96

Berbers in Morocco. These people, like some other Berbers, are nomads.* They travel about through the grasslands and desert regions of northern Africa. With some of your classmates, do research about Berbers in this book and other sources. Then draw or paint a mural showing how the Berbers meet their needs for food, clothing, and shelter. If you wish, you may also show how you think the Berbers meet their other basic needs.

language of Senegal. Swahili is a widely used language in the eastern part of Africa. (See page 46.)

Africa's people also differ in their religious beliefs. About 153 million people on this continent follow the religion of Islam.* This religion was brought to northern Africa by Arab invaders in the seventh century. Today, Moslems live mainly in Egypt, Algeria, and other countries of northern Africa. About 147 million Africans belong to various Christian churches. As you have learned, Christianity was brought to most parts of Africa by European missionaries. Most of the other people in Africa today practice animism.* Small numbers of people follow the religions of Hinduism,* Buddhism,* and Judaism.*

In Africa today, there are great differences in the ways in which people live and work. Some people live in much the same way their ancestors* did. For example, many people live in thatched houses. A few still hunt for their food with bows and arrows. However, many Africans have a way of life that is much like ours. They live in modern houses and they work in factories, shops, or offices.

Peoples of Northern Africa

To learn more about Africa's people, let's take a helicopter trip around this continent. First we shall fly over the region between the Mediterranean Sea and the Atlas Mountains. (See map on page 5.) We pass over fields, orchards, and towns in Morocco, Algeria, and Tunisia. Many of the people who live here are Berbers. They are descended from light-skinned people who lived in northern Africa thousands of years

ago. Most Berbers are farmers who live in villages. Some, however, are nomads* who live in the grasslands and desert regions of northern Africa. They move from one place to another seeking water and pasture for their flocks of sheep and goats.

Berber men, as well as women, wear long robes for protection against the hot sun. The men wear either turbans* or small, brimless, red felt hats. This kind of hat is called a fez because it was first made in the city of Fez, Morocco. Some of the women wear veils over their faces. This custom came from the Arabs, who conquered northern Africa in the seventh century. Most

of the people in northern Africa have adopted the clothing and customs of the Arabs. They follow the religion of Islam, and many of them speak the Arabic* language.

For centuries, many Arabs and Jews have lived near the northern coast of Africa. Some Arabs live in towns or in cities such as Cairo, Algiers, and Casablanca. (See Chapter 7.) Others are farmers. Many of the Jews in northern Africa are merchants or bankers. In recent years, however, many Jews have moved to Israel.*

Next, we fly to meet some of the peoples of the Sahara. Our helicopter lands near an oasis,* where a group of nomadic Berbers called the Tuaregs are camped. The Tuaregs are a tall, slender, and proud people. Although they are Moslems, we notice that the women have not adopted the custom of veiling their faces. It is the men who cover their faces with white or dark-blue veils. They wear long coats and trousers. In the past the Tuaregs were greatly feared, for they made their living by robbing desert caravans. Today, many of them are desert guides.

As we fly eastward over the Sahara, we can see that many of the people here are wandering herders. Only in very large oases is there enough water for people to settle down and grow crops.

Reaching Egypt, we look down on the great city of Cairo. (See pages 97-98.) It lies at the head of the Nile Delta. About ten million people live in Cairo, which is the largest city in Africa. However, most Egyptians are farmers. They live in the Nile Delta or in the valley of the Nile River. If the river did not provide water for irrigating their fields, their land would be a desert.

We visit a little Egyptian village along the Nile. Here we see farmers using a device called a shadoof* to lift water from the river and dump it into irrigation ditches. The water then flows through the ditches to the fields. Women with large water jars balanced on their heads walk gracefully up from the river to their homes. The thick walls of their mud-brick houses keep out much of the sun's heat.

Most Egyptians have been Moslems since the Arab invasion in the seventh century. However, some Egyptians have kept their ancient Christian faith. They belong to the Coptic Church.*

Leaving Egypt, we fly southeastward until we reach the ancient land of Ethiopia. (See map on page 5.) Here, too, most of the people are farmers. In the cool highlands, farmers grow crops such as wheat and coffee on small plots of land. In the hot, dry lowlands, nomadic herders raise sheep, goats, and other livestock. Most Ethiopians belong to the Ethiopian Christian Church, which is similar to the Coptic Church. But in the eastern part of the country, many people are Moslems.

Most Ethiopians wear clothing similar to the clothing we wear. They also often wear a large shawl called a *shamma* over their shoulders. *Shammas* are usually made of thin, white cotton cloth trimmed with bright colors.

Peoples of the Grasslands and Southern Africa

As the vegetation map on page 16 shows, much of Africa is made up of grasslands. Large parts of these grasslands are well suited to raising cattle, sheep, and goats. Many grassland people make their living by raising these animals. Others grow crops or get their food by hunting. Most grassland people make their homes in small villages. However, some live and work in large cities, such as Dakar, Nairobi, and Johannesburg.

Our helicopter takes us to a village in the grasslands of western Africa. Some of the main groups of people who live in this part of Africa are the Malinke, the Hausa, and the Fulani. In the village that we are visiting, we see men and women wearing loose-fitting

robes of white or brightly colored cloth. Some of the men wear small, round caps. The women wear colorful turbans.

The houses here have hard-mud walls and pointed, thatched roofs. A family invites us inside one of these houses. We notice that it is very clean. It has almost no furniture because most household activities are carried on outdoors. For example, members of this family cook their food over an open fire in front of their house. At night they sleep inside on woven straw mats spread on the hard earthen floor.

Division of Labor

See pages 178-181

The picture above shows the old section of Kano, a city in the grasslands of northern Nigeria. This part of Kano was built hundreds of years ago by a group of people called the Hausa. Many of the people who live here are craft workers. Some of them weave colorful cloth and rugs. Others make articles such as purses and slippers from leather. Still others carve ivory and wood into beautiful objects. Dividing up the work of a community among people who do different jobs is called division of labor. How do you suppose division of labor helps the people of Kano to meet their needs? Would it be possible to have a successful community anywhere without division of labor? Explain.

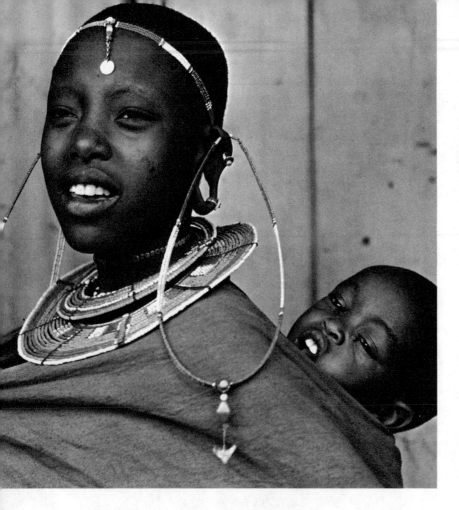

Language

See pages 178-181

A Masai mother and child in Kenya. The Masai are only one of forty different ethnic groups who make their homes in Kenya. Many of these groups have their own language. However, most of the people in Kenya also speak a language called Swahili. What problems do you think might arise if the people of Kenya did not speak a common language? How might you communicate with the people of Kenya if you went to visit them?

In nearby peanut fields, we see women working with crude, short-handled hoes. The women do all the planting and the weeding. These people move on to new land every few years, when their farmland becomes worn out.

Our journey now takes us to the grasslands of eastern Africa. Our first stop is at a Masai village in Kenya. The Masai are one of forty different ethnic groups who live in this country. As we approach the village, we notice that it is surrounded by a high wall made out of thornbushes. Inside the wall are low mud houses arranged in a circle. In the center there is a large pen for cattle.

The Masai men are tall and powerful. They usually wear a leather or cloth garment over one shoulder. The women wear much heavy jewelry on their necks, arms, and legs. The main food of the Masai is the milk and blood of their cattle. They draw the blood from the neck veins of the cattle and mix it with milk.

Next we visit the Watusi, who live in east central Africa between Lake Victoria and Lake Tanganyika. (See map on page 5.) Like the Masai, the Watusi are cattle raisers. They are among the tallest people in Africa. Some of them are about seven feet tall.

Now we fly to the Republic of South Africa to visit the Zulus. In earlier times, the Zulus were fierce warriors. Today, many of them live peacefully in farming villages called kraals. When we visit a kraal, we see that it is made up of houses arranged in a circle. The houses are round, like beehives, and are thatched with grass. In the center of the kraal is a pen where cattle are kept. Many Zulus also live in communities outside large cities such

90

as Johannesburg or Durban. There, many of them earn their living by working in mines or factories.

The Zulus speak one of many Bantu languages. (See page 44.) Bantu-speaking people make up the largest part of the population of central and southern Africa.

Our helicopter turns northwestward now. Soon we are flying over the Kalahari Desert. Here we can see some Bushmen hunters. The Bushmen are small people who live in the driest parts of southern Africa. Most of them are about five feet tall. Some Bushmen live in small groups made up of

Watusi dancers. The Watusi are a tall, proud people, famous for their dancing. These people, like the Masai, make their living by raising cattle. In what part of Africa do the Watusi live?

Bushmen hunters in the Kalahari Desert. Some of the Bushmen make their living by hunting with bows and arrows or spears, much as their ancestors did. Others work on farms or cattle ranches.

several different families. They wander from place to place over the desert and hunt animals for their food. They also gather berries, nuts, roots, and seeds. Other Bushmen earn their living by working on farms or cattle ranches.

Peoples of the Tropical Rainforest Region

Now let's visit some people in Africa's tropical rainforest. This region covers much of central Africa and also extends westward along the Gulf of Guinea. (Compare vegetation map on page 16 with map on page 5.) In the tropical rainforest region are a number of large cities. Some are river ports, like Kinshasa and Kisangani. Others are seaports, such as Lagos and Accra. Many Africans have moved to the cities in recent years. They live and work in much the same ways we do.

Other people in the tropical rainforest still live in small villages and follow their traditional way of life. We decide to visit a farming village in Zaire. The people in this village belong to a group called the Ngala. Like many other people in this part of Africa, they speak one of the Bantu languages.

To reach the Ngala village, we fly to the modern city of Kinshasa. Then we board a modern motor vessel for the journey up the Zaire River. A dense, green forest stretches along both banks of the river. The damp, low-lying land here is not suited to cattle raising. Most of the people in this region obtain their food by growing crops in forest clearings.

The village that we are visiting is built along the river. We arrive soon after a thunderstorm has passed. The sun beats down and the hot, wet earth is actually steaming. In a wide clearing are houses with mud brick walls. Some of the houses have thatched roofs that are cone-shaped to let the rain run off more quickly. Others have roofs made from sheets of metal. Like houses in the cities, many of the houses here have floors made of concrete.

The people of this village usually help each other. When someone builds a house, most of the neighbors help. Everyone in the village knows just what his or her duties are. Girls and boys carry water from the river, feed the chickens, and take care of their younger brothers and sisters. They also help their mothers weed the vegetable patches that have been cleared from the surrounding forest. We see men working beside piles of nuts that have been gathered from oil palm trees. The men are cracking the nuts open to get the kernels inside. Factories buy the kernels and extract an oil from them. Palm-kernel oil is used in making such products as soap and margarine.

In the tropical rainforest, most of the villages are near the banks of rivers or lakes. However, some people live in the deep forest. Among these people are the Pygmies. The Pygmies, who are about four and one-half feet tall, are among the smallest people in the world. They make their living by hunting. Working together, the brave Pygmy hunters kill wild animals such as elephants with knives and spears.

Europeans and Asians in Africa

In Africa today, there are several million people of European or Asian descent. However, they make up only a small part of the population of this huge continent.

When European nations ruled over most of Africa, large numbers of settlers came here from Europe. They settled mainly in places where the climate was mild and the land was good for farming. For example, many British families lived in the Eastern Highlands of Kenya. And many French people settled along the Mediterranean coast of Algeria.

Since the African countries became independent, many people of European descent have returned to their homelands. But others have remained in Africa. Usually they live in countries that were formerly ruled by the European nation from which their ancestors came. For instance, many people of British descent live in Zimbabwe.* This country used to be a colony of Great Britain.

The Republic of South Africa has the most people of European descent. Many of them are descended from Dutch settlers who came here when Holland ruled the area around Cape Town. (See page 56.) These people speak a language called Afrikaans. Afrikaans developed mainly from the Dutch language. However, it has also borrowed words from English, French, German, Malay,* and various Bantu languages. South Africa was ruled for a time by Great Britain, so many English-speaking people live here also.

In eastern Africa, there are many people whose ancestors came here in the 1800's from Asian countries such as India and Pakistan. They live mainly in seaport cities such as Durban in South Africa and Mombasa in Kenya.

(See map on page 103.) Many people of Asian descent work as shopkeepers or traders. Others work in textile mills or grow vegetables for city markets. Most of these people are followers of the Hindu religion.

Europeans of Dutch descent in the Republic of South Africa. What facts about climate, natural resources, and history help to explain why so many Europeans settled in the Republic of South Africa?

Needs

Like all other people on earth, the people of Africa have certain basic needs. They must meet these needs in order to be healthy and happy. Scientists who study human beings tell us that these basic needs are almost exactly the same for all people. It does not matter what a person's race, sex, religion, or nationality may be. He or she has the same basic needs as everyone else.

There are three kinds of basic needs. They are: physical needs, social needs, and the need for faith.

Physical Needs

Some basic needs are so important that people will die or become seriously ill if they fail to meet them. These are called physical needs. They include the need for:

1. air
2. water
3. food
4. protection from heat and cold
5. sleep and rest
6. exercise

Although all people share these needs, they do not all meet them in the same way. How do you meet your physical needs? How do you think people in Africa meet their physical needs?

Social Needs

People also have social needs. They must meet these needs in order to have a happy and useful life. Social needs include:

1. Belonging to a group. All people need to feel they belong to a group of people who respect them and whom they respect. Belonging to a family is one of the main ways people meet this need. What can the members of a family do to show that they love and respect each other? How do the members of your family help one another? Do you think family life is important to the people of Africa? Why do you think this?

Having friends also helps people meet their need for belonging to a group. What groups of friends do you have? Why are these people your friends? Do you suppose young people in Africa enjoy doing the same kinds of things with their friends as you enjoy doing with your friends? Why? Why not?

2. Goals. To be happy, every person needs goals to work for. What goals do you have? How can working toward these goals help you have a happy life? What kinds of goals do you think young people in Africa have?

3. A chance to think and learn. All people need a chance to develop and use their abilities. They need opportunities to find out about things that make them curious. What would you like to learn? How can you learn these things? How can developing your abilities help you have a happy life? Is it important for people in Africa to have a chance to think and learn? To make decisions for themselves? Why? Why not?

4. A feeling of accomplishment. You share with every other person the need for a feeling of accomplishment. All people need to feel that their lives are successful in some way. What gives you a feeling of accomplishment? Can you imagine what life would be like if you never had this feeling?

The Need for Faith

In addition to physical and social needs, all people also have a need for faith. You need to believe that life is precious and that the future is something to look forward to. You may have different kinds of faith, including the following:

1. Faith in yourself. In order to feel secure, you must have faith in your own abilities. You must feel that you will be able to do some useful work in the world and that you will be generally happy. You must believe that you can work toward solving

A Nigerian family. In what ways do members of a family often help each other meet their basic needs?

whatever problems life brings to you. How can you build faith in yourself?

2. Faith in other people. You also need to feel that you can count on other people to do their part and to help you when you need help. What people do you have faith in? What do you think life would be like without this kind of faith?

3. Faith in nature's laws. Another kind of faith that helps people face the future with confidence is faith in nature's laws. The more we learn about our universe, the more certain we feel that we can depend on nature. How would you feel if you couldn't have faith in nature's laws?

4. Religious faith. Throughout history, almost all human beings have had some kind of religious faith. Religion can help people understand themselves and the world they live in. It can bring them joy, and it can give them confidence in times of trouble. Religion can also help people live together happily. For example, most religions teach people to be honest and to love and help their neighbors. In what ways do people in Africa express their religious faith?

Many People in Africa Are Unable To Meet Their Basic Needs

The people living in Africa must meet the three kinds of basic needs we have explored here. They must meet these needs in order to have happy, useful lives. However, millions of Africa's people do not have a chance to satisfy some of their important needs. For example, large numbers of them do not have enough food to eat. Also, many Africans lack the opportunity to get a good education.

Why do you think so many people in Africa are unable to meet all of their needs? What is being done to help these people improve their way of life? This book contains much information that will help you answer these questions.

7 Cities

Africa's cities are growing rapidly. Although Africa is the second largest continent, it does not have very many large cities. There are only fourteen cities with populations of more than one million. (See map on page 103.) However, Africa's cities are growing rapidly. Each year, thousands of people leave their farming villages and come to the cities in search of a better way of life.

The rapid growth of Africa's cities has led to many problems. Most of the newcomers do not have the skills needed for good jobs in factories and offices. Also, there are not enough jobs available for everyone. Since the newcomers seldom have much money, they are forced to live in crowded slums. Chapter 13 of this book tells about some of the problems facing city dwellers in Africa today.

In spite of these problems, Africa's cities are interesting places to visit. Most of them contain a mixture of old and new ways of living. Let's explore some of these cities more closely.

Cairo. The largest city in Africa is Cairo, the capital of Egypt. About ten million people live here. Cairo lies along the Nile River, about one hundred miles from the Mediterranean Sea. At Cairo, the river valley spreads out to form the Nile Delta. In this area is some of the most fertile farmland in the world.

Shops in the old section of Cairo, Egypt. What does the picture tell you about this part of Cairo? In what ways is it like cities in the United States? In what ways is it different?

People have been living on the site of Cairo since ancient times. A few miles outside the city are the famous pyramids* and the Great Sphinx. (See picture on pages 30-31.) They were built by the Egyptians about 4,500 years ago. In A.D. 969, the Arab* rulers of Egypt founded the present city of Cairo and made it their capital.

Today Cairo is an important center of industry, trade, and education. Textile mills here make cloth from cotton grown in the Nile Valley. Other factories produce iron and steel, chemicals, paper, and sugar. Most of Egypt's large businesses have their offices in Cairo. The University of Cairo is the country's largest.

Like many cities in northern Africa, Cairo is divided into old and new sections. In the new section are modern apartment houses, hotels, stores, and government buildings. The old section resembles a storybook city of ancient times. Its narrow, crooked streets and beautiful, domed mosques* look much as they did centuries ago.

Alexandria. Egypt's leading seaport and main industrial city is Alexandria. It lies along a sheltered harbor on the Mediterranean Sea, at the western edge of the Nile Delta. This city was founded by Alexander the Great about 332 B.C. For centuries, it was a great center of wealth and learning. After the Arabs built Cairo, Alexandria became less important. By the end of the 1700's it had only a few thousand people. But it began to grow again during the 1800's. Railroad lines and a canal were built to connect it with Cairo. When the Suez Canal* was completed, Alexandria lay along the new trade route between Europe and eastern Asia. This, too, helped it to grow. Today, Alexandria is the home of more than two million people. Factories here include textile and paper mills, food canneries, and oil refineries.

Algiers. Another busy seaport on the Mediterranean is Algiers. It is Algeria's capital and largest city. About two and one-half million people live in Algiers. Outside the city is one of Algeria's richest farming areas.

Both the Phoenicians and the Romans built cities on this site long ago. The present city was founded by Berbers* in the tenth century A.D. Later it was a base for the fierce Barbary* pirates. The French began their conquest of Algeria by invading Algiers in 1830.

Algiers is built on hills that rise steeply from the seacoast. Its whitewashed buildings shine brilliantly in

*See Glossary

The modern city of Cairo lies along the banks of the Nile River. About ten million people make their homes in Cairo today. Do you think Cairo would be an interesting city to visit? Explain.

the sunlight. The modern section lies on the lower slopes of the hills, near the waterfront. On the upper slopes is the old section, known as the Casbah. Lining its narrow streets are ancient houses with balconies and tiny, barred windows.

Casablanca. The largest city in Morocco is Casablanca. It has a population of more than three million. In the early 1900's, Casablanca was only a small village on the Atlantic coast. Then the French, who ruled Morocco, began to develop a large harbor here.

Today, Casablanca is Morocco's leading seaport and manufacturing city. Among its products are textiles, metals, chemicals, and electronic* goods.

Casablanca is the most modern city in northern Africa. It has many tall, modern buildings where government officials and business people have their offices. But Casablanca also has an older section, with crowded streets and colorful bazaars.*

Lagos. Nigeria's capital and largest city is Lagos. Most of this city is built on low, flat islands along the Gulf of Guinea. (See map on page 5.) Lagos was founded several hundred years ago by the Yoruba* people. After the Portuguese arrived in the 1400's, Lagos became a center for the slave trade. The British took over Lagos in 1861. Later they made it the capital of their Nigerian colony. Today, Lagos is one of Africa's most crowded cities with more than four million people. It is Nigeria's main seaport and industrial city. Factories here make textiles, flour, cement, chemicals, and metal products. There is also an automobile assembly plant. Lagos is connected by road and railroad with other large cities in Nigeria.

Kinshasa. On the banks of the Zaire River, in the tropical rainforest of central Africa, is the city of Kinshasa. It is Zaire's capital and largest city. Kinshasa's location has made it the leading river port in Africa. Upstream from this city, the Zaire River is navigable for more than one thousand miles. But downstream are rapids and waterfalls that prevent boat travel. Goods are brought by railroad from the Atlantic coast to Kinshasa. There they are loaded onto riverboats that carry them to distant parts of the country.

A street in Lagos, the capital of Nigeria. Lagos is a busy seaport on the Gulf of Guinea. It is also Nigeria's most important manufacturing city. What are some of the main industries here?

Johannesburg is the largest city in the Republic of South Africa. What natural resources are found in the area around Johannesburg? How have these natural resources helped the city to grow?

Kinshasa was founded by the explorer Henry M. Stanley in 1887. (See page 60.) It was called Leopoldville, after King Leopold II of Belgium. The name was changed in 1966, several years after the Belgian Congo became the independent nation of Zaire.

Kinshasa has been growing rapidly in recent years. It now has about three million people. Most of Zaire's factories and business offices are in this city. The National University of Zaire is located nearby.

Johannesburg. The largest city in South Africa is Johannesburg. It lies on a hilly plateau about three hundred miles from the nearest seacoast. The area around Johannesburg, known as the Rand, has the richest gold deposits in the world. Iron ore, coal, and other valuable minerals are found here also. They provide the raw materials for many of Johannesburg's industries.

Johannesburg was founded by Afrikaners* in the 1880's when gold was first discovered in the Rand. Today it has a population of more than one and one-half million. It is one of the most modern and prosperous cities in Africa. Yet it also has some of the worst slums on the continent.

Like other South African cities, Johannesburg follows a system called apartheid.* Outside the city is a large community called Soweto, where more than one million black Africans live.

Nairobi. One of the largest cities in eastern Africa is Nairobi, the capital of Kenya. Although this city is near the equator, it lies in the Eastern Highlands about one mile above sea level. So it has a mild, pleasant climate.

Nairobi was founded in the 1890's by workers who were building a railroad from the Indian Ocean to Lake Victoria. Today, it is an important trading and manufacturing city, with about 950,000 people. Just outside Nairobi is a major coffee-growing area.

Several large wildlife reserves are located near Nairobi. Tourists from all over the world come here to see lions, elephants, and other animals roaming freely in the wilderness.

Addis Ababa. The capital and largest city of Ethiopia is Addis Ababa. About one and one-half million people live here. Addis Ababa lies on a plateau about eight thousand feet above sea level. It is connected by road and railroad with ports on the Red Sea and the Gulf of Aden. (See map on page 5.)

Addis Ababa was founded by an Ethiopian king in 1887. It has beautiful old stone churches and modern government buildings. People from every part of Ethiopia come to the marketplace here. Factories in Addis Ababa produce goods such as textiles, shoes, cement, and food products.

Nairobi, the capital of Kenya, is the center of trade and communications for much of eastern Africa. What facts about its location help to explain why it is also an important tourist center?

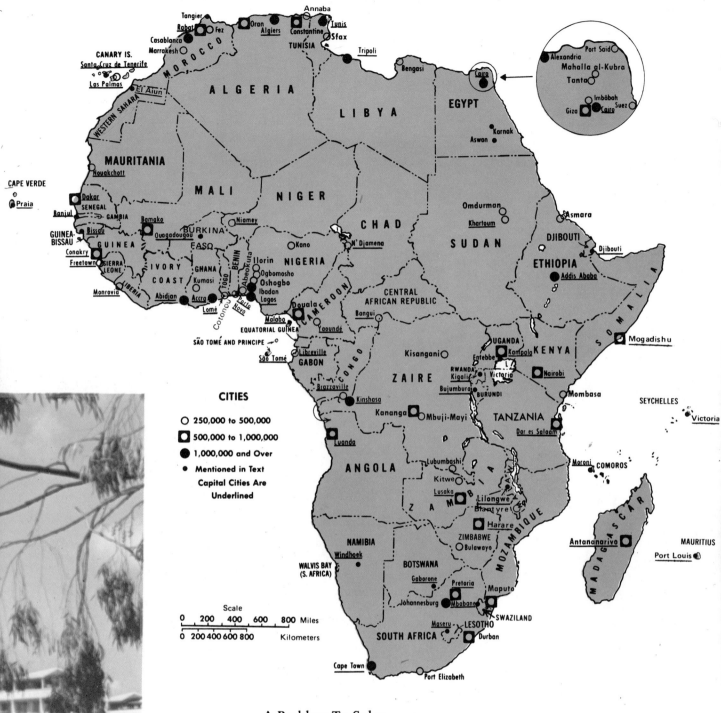

CITIES

○ 250,000 to 500,000

◧ 500,000 to 1,000,000

● 1,000,000 and Over

• Mentioned in Text
Capital Cities Are
Underlined

Scale

0   200   400   600   800 Miles

0 200 400 600 800

Kilometers

A Problem To Solve

The seven largest cities in Africa are Cairo, Alexandria, Algiers, Casablanca, Lagos, Kinshasa, and Johannesburg. (See map above.) Why did each of these great cities grow up where it did? To solve this problem, you will need to do research about each city. Then you will need to make several hypotheses. In forming your hypotheses, consider how the settlement and growth of each city has been affected by such things as:

1. its location
2. ways of earning a living
3. land and water features
4. natural resources located nearby

This book contains much information that will be helpful in solving this problem. Refer to pages 4-5 of the Skills Manual for help in finding information in other sources.

See Skills Manual, "Solving Problems"

103

8 Education

More and more of Africa's people want to go to school. However, there are not nearly enough classrooms or teachers for all the people who want to study. Only about one third of all Africans can read and write. Most countries in Africa do not have enough doctors, engineers, teachers, and other trained workers.

Today, African governments are trying hard to provide more education for their people. Many new schools have been built in recent years. A growing number of people in Africa are

Education

See pages 178-181

An elementary class in Liberia. Many people in Africa have never had an opportunity to receive an education. Today, about two thirds of all Africans still do not know how to read or write. However, most African countries are working very hard to provide more schools and teachers for their people. To understand more fully why education is so important to people in Africa, discuss the following questions as a class.

1. Why do you suppose so many people in Africa would like to go to school?
2. How does education help people to meet their need for food, clothing, and shelter?
3. How does education help people to reach their goals in life?
4. Do you think you could ever reach your goals if you were unable to read and write? Explain your answer.

learning to read and write. They are also learning modern methods of farming, as well as the special skills needed for jobs in business, industry, and government.

Although many African children do not go to school, they still receive some education. Many of them learn the history and laws of their ethnic* group from older people in their village. Children are taught to be honest and brave and to respect their parents and neighbors. They learn much through songs, stories, and dances. As African children work alongside their parents, they learn the tasks of daily living. For example, they may learn how to hunt, fish, farm, or keep house.

*See Glossary

Moslem* schools. Many people in Africa who are Moslems send their children to special religious schools. Let us visit one of these schools in Morocco. Here we see students sitting cross-legged on mats on the tiled floor. They bend over their tablets as they learn to read and write the Arabic language. This is the language in which the Koran, the holy book of Islam, is written. In addition to reading and writing, these children study Moslem law and religion.

There are several Moslem colleges and universities in northern Africa. In Cairo is al-Azhar University, which was founded about A.D. 970. It is one of the oldest universities in the world.

Christian mission schools. Among the first people to establish schools in Africa were Christian missionaries from the United States and Europe. Today, some of these schools are still in operation. Many Africans who have become doctors, lawyers, engineers, and government leaders began their education in mission schools.

Public schools. The number of children in Africa's public schools has increased greatly in recent years. Today, in Tunisia, about eight out of ten children attend elementary school. However, in much of Africa many children still cannot go to school. In Upper Volta (Burkina Faso), for example, only about one child out of ten attends elementary school. In Africa as a whole, about fifteen out of every one hundred children receive a high school

A home economics class in Nigeria. In some African schools, students learn sewing and other homemaking skills. How do you think such skills might help them meet their needs?

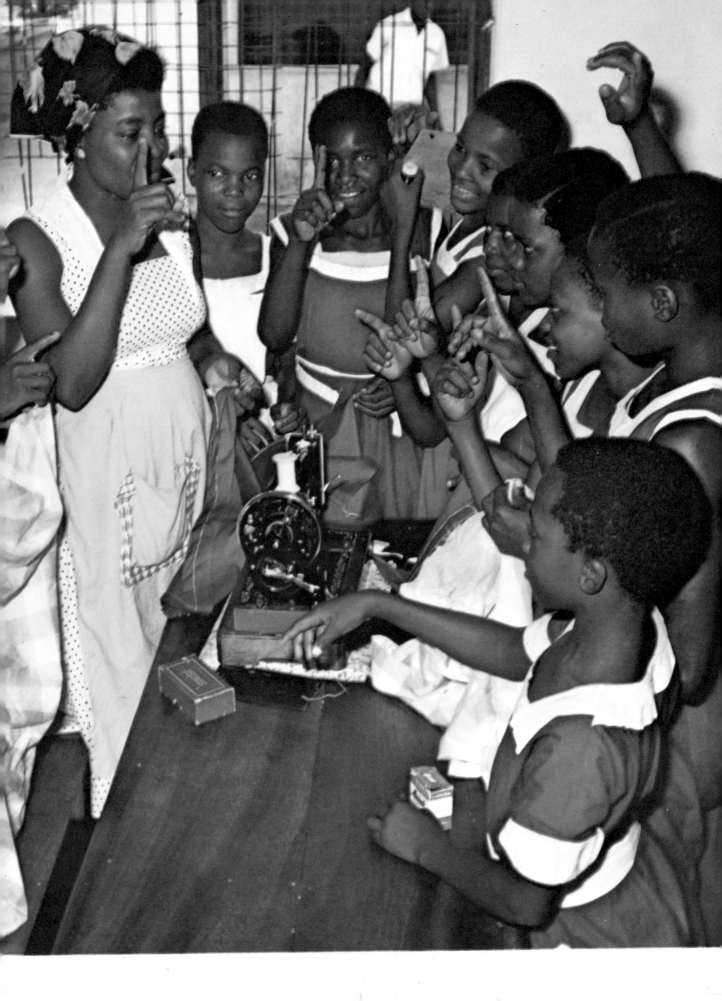

education. Governments in Africa need to provide more schools, textbooks, and trained teachers.

Technical schools. Africa needs more schools where young people may learn technical skills that will help them obtain jobs. Some African countries have already built many technical schools. In Ivory Coast, for instance, there are schools where students can learn woodworking, mechanics, and other useful skills. In Libya, the United Nations helped to start a training center where typing, bookkeeping, and other office skills are taught.

Universities. Africa does not have enough colleges and universities for all the people who would like to obtain a higher education. In recent years, however, many African countries have built new universities or enlarged those they already had. For example, twenty-three of Nigeria's twenty-four universities have been established since 1960. More than 93,000 students now attend universities in Nigeria. The Republic of Zaire has combined all of its institutions of higher learning into a single national university, with campuses in three separate locations.

High school students in Tanzania. These students are attending a school that was built with the help of the International Development Association.* In Africa, only about fifteen out of every one hundred students receive a high school education. What do you think are the reasons for this?

Making Discoveries

A great number of Africa's people are Moslems, or followers of the religion of Islam. Do research about Islam and write a report about this religion to share with your class. Include the following information in your report:

1. when, where, and how Islam was founded
2. other parts of the world to which it has spread
3. some of its important teachings
4. some customs and beliefs of its followers

Pages 4-8 of the Skills Manual contain suggestions that will be helpful in finding information and in writing your report. To make your report more interesting, you may wish to include the following:

a. a map showing the parts of the world where Islam is important today
b. pictures of mosques, or Moslem temples of worship
c. pictures of famous Moslem leaders

Explore One of Africa's Cities

Africa's large cities are interesting and fascinating places to visit. Investigate one of the cities listed below:

Casablanca   Addis Ababa   Lagos
Kinshasa   Alexandria   Algiers

As you do research, imagine you are visiting this city. Now, write a letter to a friend about what you have discovered. In your letter, you may want to include information about the following:

1. the location and population of the city
2. history of the city or the area in which it is located
3. places of interest in or near the city
4. some important facts about the city today

In addition to this book, you will need to refer to other sources. Pages 4-5 of the Skills Manual contain helpful suggestions for finding information.

Build a Model of Kano

Part of the city of Kano, in northern Nigeria, was built hundreds of years ago. Form a committee with some of your classmates to make a model of the old walled section of this city. Use the picture on page 89 as a guide for making your model. Other students may wish to form a committee to make a mural that shows daily life in Kano. When your project has been completed, share it with other classes in your school. Pages 9-10 of the Skills Manual contain some helpful suggestions for working together.

Prepare a Television Interview

With another member of your class, choose a country in Africa and do research about the people who live there. Then, imagine that one of you is a television interviewer and the other is a citizen of the country you have chosen. Prepare a script for a television program in which the team member being interviewed describes what the people of that country are like. In your script, you may wish to include information about:

1. the main ethnic groups
2. clothing
3. shelter
4. religion
5. life in a village
6. life in a city
7. earning a living

Perform your television interview for your class. Your performance will be more interesting if you illustrate your interview with pictures and a map of the country you choose.

Learn From a Guest Speaker

In recent years, many students from Africa have come to study in the United States. Perhaps there are African students living in your community or nearby. If so, invite one of them to talk to your class. Ask this person to tell about the school system in his or her country. Be sure to take notes during the talk. Also jot down some important questions about education that you would like to ask your guest after the talk. Later, as a class, discuss how education in your guest's country compares with education in the United States.

Part 4
Earning a Living

If you were to visit Africa, you would see many people who make their living by raising livestock or growing crops. In what other ways do you suppose people in Africa earn their living? As you do research in Part 4, try to answer the following questions.

- What are the leading farm products of Africa? In what parts of the continent is each product raised? What factors help determine the kinds of crops and livestock raised in each area?
- What are some of the important natural resources of Africa? In what parts of Africa are these natural resources found? How do the people of Africa make use of these resources?
- What are Africa's leading industries? Why does Africa have few modern industries?
- What forms of transportation do the people of Africa use? Why are the governments of most African countries trying to improve their transportation and communication systems?
- What problems of development do the people of Africa face? In what ways are they trying to solve these problems?

Using Natural Resources

See pages 178-181

Farming in Nigeria. Farming is the main way in which the people of Africa make their living. What natural resources do farmers use? Are these natural resources available in all parts of Africa? Explain your answer. What can be done to help farmers in areas that lack these natural resources?

9 Farming

Most Africans make their living by raising livestock or growing crops. Many of these farmers are very poor. Except on large farms and plantations, very little modern farm machinery is used in Africa. People cultivate their fields with hoes or wooden plows pulled by oxen. With these old-fashioned tools, one person cannot raise much food. Let's discover more about farming in different parts of Africa.

Farming along the northwestern coast. There are many fertile farms along the northwestern coast of Africa. During the mild winter season, enough rain falls here to grow many crops. Streams from the Atlas Mountains provide water for irrigation during the hot summer.

Plowing a field in Morocco. There are many fertile farms along Africa's northwestern coast. What facts about the climate of this region help to explain why crops grow so well here?

We see different kinds of crops as we drive eastward along this coast. Wheat, barley, and oats grow in many of the fields we pass. Green vineyards and groves of orange, lemon, and olive trees cover much of the countryside. In the hills, boys are tending herds of cattle, sheep, and goats.

Farming in Egypt.* After we arrive in Egypt, we take a boat up the mighty Nile River. Bordering this river is one of the most densely populated farming

*See Glossary

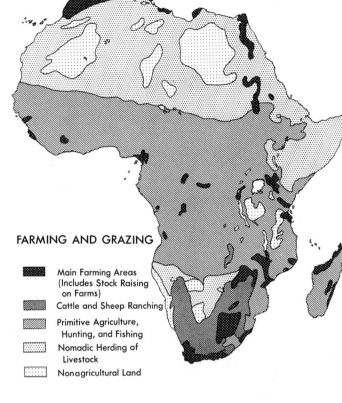

FARMING AND GRAZING

▓	Main Farming Areas (Includes Stock Raising on Farms)
▨	Cattle and Sheep Ranching
▧	Primitive Agriculture, Hunting, and Fishing
░	Nomadic Herding of Livestock
⬚	Nonagricultural Land

Land use in Africa. Many parts of Africa are not well suited to farming. Why is this so?

A Problem To Solve

It is very difficult for many farmers in Africa to make a good living from the land. Why is this true? In forming hypotheses to solve this problem, consider how farming is affected by:

a. the land and water features of Africa

b. the climate here

c. the size of farms in Africa

d. methods and tools used by Africans

e. government

Chapters 1,2,and **13** also contain information that will be helpful in solving this problem.

See Skills Manual, "Solving Problems"

A sugarcane harvest, along the Nile River in Egypt. The densely populated Nile Valley in Egypt is one of the most fertile farming areas in the world. Why are most of the farms located here very small?

regions in the world, the Nile Valley. Because the land here is divided among many people, most of the farms are very small. Farmers in the Nile Valley use water from the river to irrigate their land. The most important crop they raise is cotton. Corn is another valuable crop. In addition, Egyptian farmers raise

Desert pasturelands. Leaving the Nile Valley, we join a camel caravan that is traveling through the Sahara. (See map on page 5.) Soon the caravan stops near a "tent village" of wandering desert people. We notice that they have set their tents near shrubs and grasses, which furnish food for their flocks. Boys are guarding the sheep, goats, and camels. Women of the tribe are making blankets, tents, and rugs from wool. The desert people trade some of these products for dates and vegetables in market towns and oases. Much of their food, however, consists of meat, cheese, and camel's milk from their herds. They cannot grow the other food they need, because there is too little water in the desert.

Farming in the northern grasslands. We leave the desert now and travel into the grasslands of northern Africa. (See vegetation map on page 16.) Here we find that rainfall and wells provide enough water for some farming. Many native African farmers own their farms, and others work on farms that are owned by Europeans. The usual crops raised here are millet,* wheat, corn, cotton, sorghum,* and peanuts.

In a nearby farming village, we see a group of villagers listening to a government farming expert. The villagers are learning how to improve their methods of farming. The farming expert tells them to raise "cash crops," such as peanuts. These are crops the farmers can sell so they will have money to buy the things they need.

Sheep, cattle, and goats are also raised in the grasslands. In parts of this region, however, disease-carrying insects called tsetse flies make it impossible to keep certain kinds of livestock. The bite of some of these flies causes sleeping

wheat, rice, sugarcane, and beans. Instead of tractors, they often use farm animals such as oxen and water buffalo to pull their plows.

sickness in people and a disease called nagana* in livestock. Only goats and a type of dwarf cattle can be raised.

Farming in the rainforest. Now we travel to the city of Abidjan, in the country of Ivory Coast. Abidjan lies in the tropical rainforest region of central Africa. (Compare vegetation map on page 16 with map on page 5.) Outside Abidjan, we see many small farms on which cacao trees are grown. Seeds from these trees are used in making cocoa and chocolate. The hot, moist climate of the rainforest is good for growing cacao. Ivory Coast, Ghana, and Nigeria are among the world's leading producers of this crop.

During our visit to the rainforest, we also see many oil* palm trees. Valuable oils are obtained from the fruit and kernels of these trees. These oils are used in making soap, candles, margarine, and other products.

Many other important crops are grown in the rainforest region. Among these are coffee, bananas, cotton, and pineapples. Some crops are grown on small farms, while others are raised on large plantations. In Liberia and Zaire, there are large plantations of rubber trees. A liquid called latex, taken from the bark of these trees, is used in making rubber.

All of these crops are grown mainly for sale to other countries. But farmers in the rainforest also grow crops for their own use. For example, large amounts of yams* and manioc* are grown for food. The plantain, a type

Bananas are grown on plantations in Africa's rainforest region. What are some of the other crops that are grown in this part of Africa?

of banana, is also important here. Plantains are not as sweet as the bananas we eat in the United States. The African people cook plantains and use them as a vegetable.

Farming in the highlands of eastern Africa. When we visit the highlands of eastern Africa, we see many more farms. Even though this part of Africa is near the equator, it is so high above sea level that the climate is seldom hot. Enough rain falls for crops to grow well.

Our first stop in the Eastern Highlands is Ethiopia. (See map on page 5.) This is the country where coffee was first discovered. Today, coffee is Ethiopia's most important cash crop. In addition, farmers here raise wheat, corn, cotton, barley, and livestock.

Next we visit the farming and grazing lands of Kenya. Many people in this region keep herds of cattle. In fact, some of them make their living almost entirely by raising cattle. We

Farming in Kenya. Much of the Eastern Highlands region is well suited to farming. The soil here is good for growing many different crops. What additional facts about the land and climate of this region help explain why farming is so successful here?

Exchange

See pages 178-181

Harvesting sisal* in Kenya. The workers shown in this picture do not grow their own food. Instead, they earn their living by harvesting sisal. How do you suppose these workers obtain the food they and their families need? Could they meet their needs without the great idea of exchange? Explain.

see many small farms, as well as a number of large plantations. Some of the plantations are owned by people whose ancestors came from Britain when Kenya was a British colony.

Many different kinds of crops are grown in the Eastern Highlands of Kenya. Among these crops are coffee, tea, sisal,* pyrethrum,* corn, wheat, and sugarcane. Some of the farm products raised in Kenya are used by people in this country. The rest are exported to other parts of the world.

Farming in southern Africa. From Kenya we fly to Zimbabwe, in southern Africa. Here we see many fields of tobacco, cotton, coffee, tea, and sugarcane. These crops are grown mainly for export. Farmers grow such crops as corn, wheat, and sorghum for food.

The final stop on our journey is the Republic of South Africa. Many different kinds of farming are carried on in this country. In the hot, humid lowlands along the Indian Ocean, there are large sugarcane plantations. In the cooler highlands, we see large fields of corn and wheat. We also see many dairy farms and cattle ranches. Sheep and goats are raised in places that are too dry or rugged for growing crops. To the west is the Kalahari Desert. (See map on page 5.) Much of this region is too dry for farming.

In the area around Cape Town, the climate is much like it is along the northwestern coast of Africa. Winters are mild and rainy, and summers are dry. Here we see apple orchards, vineyards, and groves of orange trees.

Picking tea leaves on a plantation in Mozambique. There is much good farmland in eastern and southern Africa. What kinds of crops and livestock are raised here? How are these farm products used?

A worker sorting diamonds in the Republic of South Africa. Diamonds are one of Africa's most important mineral resources. What other minerals do African mines produce in large quantities?

10   Natural Resources

One day in 1866, a farmer's child was walking along the banks of the Orange River in southern Africa. (See map on page 5.) This small child found a strange pebble and picked it up. People wondered what it was, but few of them thought it was very important. Imagine their surprise to learn that it was a diamond worth $2,500! Two years later, a young shepherd in southern Africa found another diamond. This one was worth $55,000.

The discovery of diamonds in southern Africa brought thousands of trea-sure hunters to the region. In time they dug deep diamond mines. Today about three fourths of the world's diamonds are mined in Africa. The finest stones are carefully cut to make sparkling gems for jewelry. Diamonds that are dark colored or imperfect are used to make tools such as drills. This is be-cause diamonds are so hard they can cut through all kinds of rock and metal.

Africa is a treasure house of minerals. Af-rica produces many other minerals be-sides diamonds. The map on page 123 shows where various kinds of minerals are found. About two thirds of the world's gold is mined in Africa. So is about two thirds of the world's cobalt.* Africa is a major producer of copper, manganese,* chromium,* antimony,* and platinum.* It also produces much tin, bauxite,* asbestos,* and phosphate* rock. All of these minerals are highly useful to industry. A large amount of uranium* comes from African mines. This mineral is used as a fuel in producing atomic energy.

Two important energy fuels found in Africa are petroleum, or oil, and natural gas. Nigeria and Libya are among the world's leading producers of oil. Several other African countries also have large deposits of this mineral. Natural gas is usually found in the same places as oil.

Coal, also an energy fuel, and iron ore are two other important resources of Africa. Both of these minerals are needed for making iron and steel. In

*See Glossary

Oil workers in Libya. Two countries in Africa, Libya and Nigeria, are among the world's leading producers of petroleum. Compare the map on the opposite page with the map on page 5 to discover what other African countries or territories have deposits of petroleum.

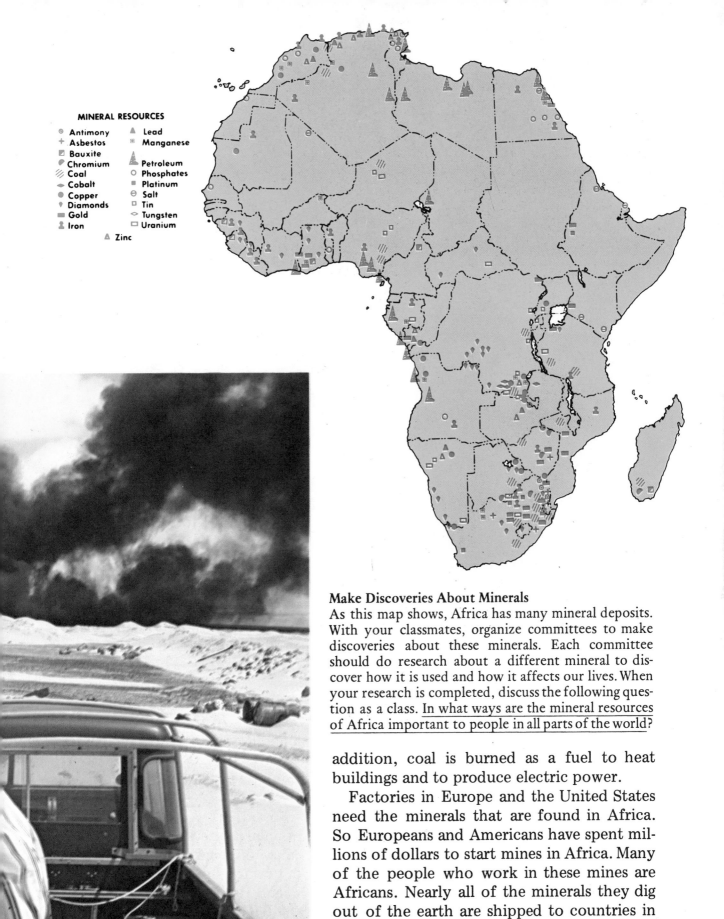

MINERAL RESOURCES

- ⊙ Antimony
- + Asbestos
- ▨ Bauxite
- Chromium
- ▨ Coal
- Cobalt
- ● Copper
- ▾ Diamonds
- ▬ Gold
- ⚥ Iron
- ▲ Lead
- ▧ Manganese
- ⛰ Petroleum
- ○ Phosphates
- Platinum
- ⊖ Salt
- ▫ Tin
- ◇ Tungsten
- ▢ Uranium
- △ Zinc

Make Discoveries About Minerals

As this map shows, Africa has many mineral deposits. With your classmates, organize committees to make discoveries about these minerals. Each committee should do research about a different mineral to discover how it is used and how it affects our lives. When your research is completed, discuss the following question as a class. In what ways are the mineral resources of Africa important to people in all parts of the world?

addition, coal is burned as a fuel to heat buildings and to produce electric power.

Factories in Europe and the United States need the minerals that are found in Africa. So Europeans and Americans have spent millions of dollars to start mines in Africa. Many of the people who work in these mines are Africans. Nearly all of the minerals they dig out of the earth are shipped to countries in other parts of the world.

123

Miners drilling for gold in a mine in Ghana. Africa produces about two thirds of the world's gold.

Mining regions of Africa. One of Africa's most important mining regions is located in the Republic of South Africa. (Compare the map on page 123 with the map on page 5.) Let's visit one of the large gold mines near the city of Johannesburg. An elevator carries us thousands of feet below the surface of the earth. Here we see miners drilling for gold in tunnels where the temperature is always about 110° F. More gold is produced in the region around Johannesburg than in any other part of the world.

South Africa produces many other minerals besides gold. It leads the world in the production of gem diamonds and chromium, and is also a leading producer of manganese, uranium, platinum, antimony, and asbestos. It produces more coal and iron ore than any other African country.

When we travel northward, we come to another rich mining region. It lies along both sides of the border between Zambia and Zaire. Here there are huge deposits of copper and cobalt. Zaire and Zambia are leading producers of both these metals. Other mineral resources found here include uranium, zinc, and manganese.

The map on page 123 shows that other important mining regions lie in western and northern Africa. Liberia has rich deposits of iron ore, while Guinea is a major producer of bauxite.

**Using
Tools**

See pages 178-181

Because Africa has so many rich mineral deposits, mining is important in several parts of the continent. Miners use many different kinds of tools in order to dig the ore from the mines and carry it up to the surface of the earth. What kinds of tools do you suppose the miners shown in the pictures on these two pages are using? What tasks do you think they are accomplishing with these tools? Do you think it would be possible for workers in Africa and other parts of the world to mine large quantities of ore if they didn't have these powerful tools to work with? Give reasons for your answer.

Hauling copper ore in a Zambia copper mine. Copper is Zambia's most important export product.

Some of the world's largest deposits of phosphate rock are located in Morocco and Tunisia.

Forest resources of Africa. The vast forests of Africa provide other valuable natural resources. Loggers in the tropical rainforest region cut down hardwood trees, such as mahogany and ebony. This wood is shipped to mills and factories in other parts of the world. There it is used to make lumber, furniture, and other products. Logging is costly and difficult in Africa's rainforest, however. More good roads and railroads are needed to transport the logs to the ports along the coast.

Using
Natural
Resources

See pages 178-181

Logging in the tropical rainforest in the Central African Republic. Forests are important to people everywhere. They provide valuable natural resources from which thousands of products are made. In addition, forests help to conserve soil, water, and wildlife. Do research about forests and forest products in other sources. Then, use your imagination to complete one of the following projects.

1. Write a story about what your life might be like if you could not use products made from forest resources. Share the story with your classmates.
2. Draw pictures or cartoons of what the earth might look like if all of the world's forests had been destroyed. Share your drawings with your class.

Kariba Dam on the Zambezi River in southern Africa. Waterpower is one of Africa's most important resources. Why has so little of this waterpower been used to produce electricity?

Waterpower. One of the most important natural resources of Africa is waterpower. This vast continent has enough waterpower to produce more than one third of the world's hydroelectricity. Until recently, however, little of this waterpower was used. It is very expensive to build the dams and power plants needed to produce hydroelectricity.

Today, Africa is beginning to develop more of its waterpower. A huge dam has been built on the Nile River at Aswan, in Egypt. The Aswan High Dam helps to control floods on the Nile and to supply hydroelectricity. It also provides water to help irrigate about two million acres of farmland.

Several other large dams have been built or are now under construction in Africa. For example, there are two large dams on the Zambezi River. One is the great Kariba Dam, along the border between Zambia and Zimbabwe. The other is the Cabora Bassa Dam in Mozambique. Akosombo Dam on the Volta River supplies electric power for homes and factories throughout Ghana. Another huge dam, the Inga Dam, has been built on the Zaire River, in Zaire.

Fisheries. Many different kinds of fish live in the waters that surround the continent of Africa. Tuna, sardines, and other fish are caught in the Atlantic Ocean off Africa's northwestern coast. Sponges are collected along the Mediterranean coast. Lobster, anchovies, mackerel, and other seafood are caught off the Atlantic coast of southwestern Africa. Some of the fish are eaten fresh by Africa's people. Some are canned, dried, or smoked, and exported to other parts of the world. Fish from lakes and rivers also provide food for the African people.

11 Industry

Africa's rich mines and forests produce many raw materials for industry. However, in most of this huge continent there are few mills and factories. Only a small number of Africans make their living in industry. Most are farmers and herders. They do not have the education and skills they need to develop modern industries. They do not have the money or equipment, either.

African craft workers make many beautiful and useful articles. Skillful craft workers make by hand many of the tools, household goods, and other things which Africa's people use. Let's see some of these people at work. First we walk through the old shopping district of Cairo, Egypt.* To one side of us is a group of tentmakers, sitting cross-legged on mats. They are embroidering tent linings and wall decorations. Farther on, we enter a shop where artists are painting tiles. These will be used to decorate the floors and walls of homes and shops. In the next street we can hear the hammer blows of metalworkers. They are making designs on articles of brass, copper, or silver.

Next we visit the city of Rabat in Morocco. Here we see craft workers making soft slippers, beautiful book covers, and other articles of leather.

*See Glossary

An Egyptian craft worker making pottery. Although African craft workers make many beautiful and useful articles, they cannot produce all the things needed for a modern way of life. Why do you think this is so?

Some of the world's finest handmade leather goods come from Morocco.

In the country of Senegal, we see a group of villagers making a dugout canoe. They hollow out a big log with fire. Then they shape it with tools that were probably made by the village blacksmith. The blacksmith usually has a forge near his mud-brick house. Here he makes spearheads, iron tools, and other articles the people need.

Craft workers cannot produce the things needed for a modern way of life. Although African craft workers make many useful and beautiful articles, they cannot make the tractors, electric power generators, hospital equipment, and other things the Africans need in order to have a modern way of life. To produce these things, Africans need to develop modern industries.

There is another reason why Africa needs industry. As long as most of the people are farmers or herders who raise only as much as they and their families need, they will be very poor. When more factories are built, however, more people will be able to have jobs in which they can earn money. Then they will be able to afford the things they want and need in order to have a healthier and more modern way of life.

People from other parts of the world are helping Africans develop the industries they need. Foreign companies are establishing factories in Africa. Countries such as the United States are lending money and sending engineers and other skilled workers to African countries that request them. The United Nations is helping also.

What modern industries does Africa have? As we travel through Africa, we find two main kinds of modern industries. One kind prepares raw materials taken from African mines, forests, and farms for sale to other countries. The other kind produces cloth and other manufactured goods for the people of Africa to use. Let's find out where

these industries are located and see some of them for ourselves.

The Republic of South Africa is one of the most highly industrialized countries in Africa. It produces nearly all of the manufactured goods its people need. South Africa has many of the raw materials needed for manufacturing. (Compare the map on page 123 with the map on page 135.) It also has many skilled workers that are needed by industry.

Workers assembling radios in the Republic of South Africa. This country is one of the most highly industrialized nations on the African continent. What facts help explain why this is so?

An automobile-assembly plant in Algeria. Modern industries have been established along Africa's northwestern coast. Factories here produce iron and steel, textiles, chemicals, and other products.

As we travel through South Africa, we see many large mines that produce minerals, such as antimony* and manganese,* for industry. We also visit factories that manufacture explosives and equipment used in these mines. Some factories in this country produce clothing and process foods. Among the other kinds of factories here are steel mills and automobile-assembly plants.

In the rich mining region that lies on both sides of the border between Zam-bia and the Republic of Zaire, we see many modern industrial plants. Smelters have been built here, in which rocks containing copper are melted. The copper is made into long bars. These are shipped to countries in other parts of the world, where they are used in factories that make electric wire and other copper products.

To the northeast, in the country of Kenya, we visit factories where leaves from sisal* plants are processed to

What are the names of five countries along Africa's northern coast in which modern industries have been established? The maps on pages 5 and 135 will help you answer this question.

make rope. Sisal is grown on many plantations in this region. Much of it is sold to other countries.

Other industries are being established in Kenya and neighboring regions in eastern Africa. We visit several factories where products such as blankets, shoes, fertilizer, and paint are made to sell to the people who live there. Other factories use forest resources to produce building materials and furniture. There are also large food-processing plants that produce flour, sugar, soft drinks, and other products.

When we travel to Egypt, we find that here, too, people are working hard to establish modern industry. We visit oil refineries, an iron and steel mill, and several modern textile factories. In other plants we see workers making cement, drugs, or fertilizer.

In the cities along the northwestern coast of Africa, there are also modern industries. During our visit, we tour automobile-assembly plants and factories where farm machinery and chemicals are manufactured.

Industry is also developing rapidly in Nigeria and other countries along the continent's western coast. When we travel to the port city of Lagos, in Nigeria, we see many huge tanks that are used for storing petroleum products. Nigeria is one of the world's leading producers and exporters of petroleum. We also visit modern plants where furniture, textiles, soap, and paper are made. In other factories, workers are assembling automobiles, bicycles, radio equipment, and sewing machines.

When we leave these modern plants, however, we walk past small workshops like those we read about in the beginning of this chapter. These remind us that Africa does not yet have nearly as much modern industry as it needs. It will take hard work and the help of people from foreign countries to bring a better way of life to the people of this great continent.

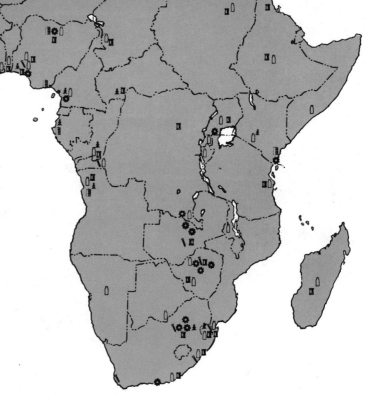

INDUSTRIES

- \ Chemical Products
- ▯ Food Products
- ☘ Forest Products
- ✿ Metal Products
- ▮ Petroleum Products
- ◫ Textiles and Clothing

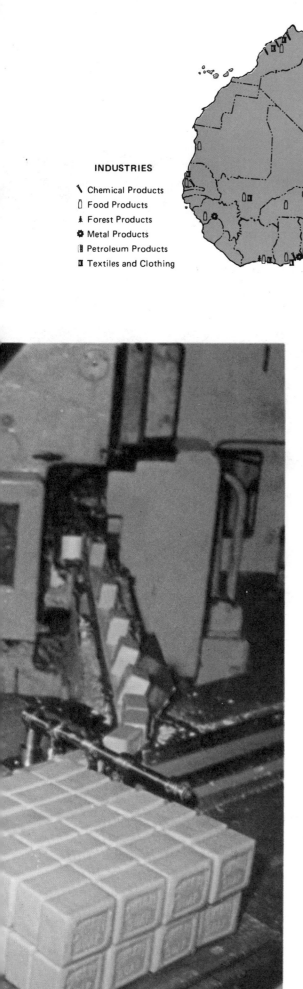

Make Discoveries With Maps

The map above shows where modern industry has been established in Africa. Discover answers to the following questions by comparing this map with the map on page 5.

1. Which countries have <u>some</u> modern industries?
2. Which African countries have <u>no</u> modern industries?
3. In which countries are petroleum products manufactured?
4. In which countries are metal products manufactured?

Division of Labor

See pages 178-181

The woman shown in the picture at left works in a soap factory in Nigeria. Unlike most of the people who live in Africa, this woman does not grow her own food on a farm. Instead, she earns her living by working in an industrial plant. What are some ways in which Africans earn their living besides working on farms and in factories? Do you think it would be possible to have modern industry in Africa or in any other part of the world without division of labor? Explain your answer.

A riverboat on the Zaire (Congo) River. The Zaire is the most important waterway in Africa. What are the reasons for this? What other forms of transportation do people in Africa use?

12 Transportation and Communication

Most African countries have not yet developed good systems of transportation. In most parts of Africa today, there is a lack of good transportation. Many areas are not served by paved roads or by railroads. Water travel is often slow and inconvenient. Air travel is fast, but it is expensive. When Africans want to go from one place to another, they still often travel on foot.

Several facts help explain why there is a lack of good transportation in Africa. As you know, this huge continent is more than three times the size of the United States. Most of Africa's cities and large towns are many miles apart. It costs a great deal of money to build roads and railroads over these vast distances. At the same time, most African countries are very poor. They do not have enough money to build all the roads and railroads they need.

Land features have held back the growth of transportation in many parts of Africa. This continent is made up largely of a high plateau. Steep slopes

A Problem To Solve

In Africa today, it is often difficult to travel from one place to another. Why have most African countries been unable to develop good systems of transportation? As you form hypotheses to solve this problem, you will want to consider facts about:

1. the land and water features of Africa
2. the climate and vegetation in Africa
3. Africa's natural resources
4. European influence in Africa
5. recent problems of development in Africa

Other chapters of this book also contain information that will be helpful in solving this problem.

See Skills Manual, "Solving Problems"

lie between the plateau and the narrow plains that border Africa's coasts. It is hard to build roads and railroads up these slopes. In other parts of Africa, there are rugged mountains and deep canyons that serve as barriers to transportation.

The climate of Africa has also had a harmful effect on transportation. Most of northern Africa is covered by the great desert called the Sahara. Travel over the Sahara is difficult because of the heat, the lack of water, and the drifting sand. In much of central Africa, the climate is hot and damp. Here there are swamps and dense forests that make it hard to build roads and railroads. Sometimes heavy rains wash away the roads or the railroad beds.

There are also obstacles to water travel in Africa. This continent has several large rivers that can be used as waterways. But most of these rivers are interrupted by rapids or shallow places where boats cannot travel. The coasts of Africa do not have many deep bays that make good harbors for ships. Also, fierce storms often strike the African coasts in certain places. These storms can make ocean travel difficult and dangerous.

Another problem facing transportation in Africa is a lack of cheap fuel. As you know, gasoline or some other fuel made from petroleum is needed to run cars, trucks, ships, and airplanes. Locomotives usually burn coal or fuel oil. Most African countries do not have large deposits of coal or petroleum. They must buy the fuels they need from other countries. Today, imported fuels are usually very costly.

Transportation is improving in Africa. In spite of these problems, Africa's people are now developing better systems of transportation. Each year they are building more roads and railroads. They are also improving harbors and airports. Much of this work they are doing themselves. But they have also received help from other countries such as the United States, China, and Great Britain.

Roads. Today there are more than 800,000 miles of roads in Africa. However, only about 60,000 miles of roads are paved with concrete or other hard materials. The rest are mostly dirt roads or narrow trails. In dry weather, these roads are bumpy and dusty. In wet weather, they are often so muddy that they cannot be used.

Most of the good roads in Africa are located in only a few areas. (See map on opposite page.) For example, South Africa has a large network of highways. The land and climate of that country are quite favorable for road building. There are also a number of good roads near the Mediterranean coast in Morocco, Algeria, and Tunisia.

Some parts of Africa have hardly any roads at all. One of these areas is the Sahara Desert. Only a few roads that cross the Sahara can be used by cars and trucks. But there are a number of caravan routes, which are used by people traveling with camels. Camels are well suited to desert travel. They can go swiftly over long distances without needing much food or water.

If you were to drive along a highway in Africa, you would see many different forms of transportation. Many Africans ride bicycles or travel on foot. Some ride on the backs of donkeys or other animals. Others travel in wagons pulled by donkeys or oxen. In the

A busy street in Lagos, Nigeria. Most people in Africa today do not have cars of their own. Why is this so? How many different kinds of transportation can you find in the picture below?

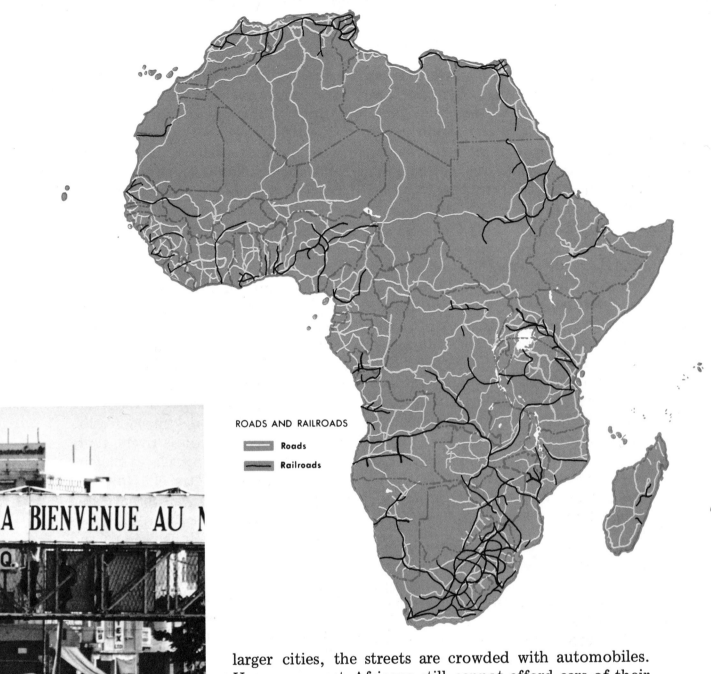

ROADS AND RAILROADS

▭ Roads
━ Railroads

larger cities, the streets are crowded with automobiles. However, most Africans still cannot afford cars of their own. If they want to travel long distances, they usually go by bus or train. Today, more and more trucks are being used to carry goods on African streets and highways.

Railroads. Africa has about 50,000 miles of railroads. This may seem like a large number, but it is not so large when compared to other parts of the world. For example, the United States has about four times as many miles of railroads as Africa does.

The map above shows where Africa's main railroads are located. South Africa has the largest railroad network on the continent. People can travel on fast, modern trains between the main cities of the country. South Africa's railroads connect with other lines in neighboring countries, such as Zimbabwe, Mozambique, and Botswana. It is now possible to go by train across southern Africa from the Atlantic Ocean to the Indian Ocean. There are also railroad networks in the Nile Delta* of Egypt and in Tunisia, Algeria, and Morocco.

On the map, you can see many railroads extending a short distance inland from the African coasts. Most of these lines were built when European nations ruled over a large part of Africa. The Europeans were eager to get raw materials such as farm crops, forest products, and minerals. They built railroads to carry these goods from the places where they were produced to seaports along the coasts. Today, many of these lines are still in operation. Little has been done to connect them with one another in order to form larger railroad networks.

Rivers and lakes. As you have discovered, Africa has several large rivers that can be used for transportation. Among these are the Zaire, the Nile, the Niger, and the Zambezi.

The most important waterway in Africa is the Zaire River, formerly known as the Congo. The Zaire and its tributaries* flow through a part of Africa where the climate is very hot and moist. Dense forests and swamps cover much of the land, making it difficult to build roads and railroads. For this reason, water travel is especially important here. Boats can travel on the Zaire and its tributaries for about six thousand miles. These boats range in size from dugout canoes to large motor vessels. In some places, there are rapids and waterfalls that interfere with boat travel.

Railroads have been built to carry goods and passengers around the parts of the river that are not navigable.*

For thousands of years, the Nile River has been a major transportation route for people in Egypt and the Sudan. Today there are a number of good roads and railroads in the Nile Valley. As a result, water transportation is less important than it used to be. However, many sailboats and small motor vessels still travel up and down the Nile River. They carry mostly bulky farm crops, such as cotton and grain. Passenger boats travel on Lake Nasser, which was formed by building the huge Aswan High Dam across the Nile River.

The Niger and Zambezi rivers are not as important as transportation routes. On both of these rivers, there are rapids and shallow places that interfere with water travel. However, many small boats travel on navigable stretches of the Niger River. They carry farm products such as peanuts and palm oil to market.

Some of Africa's large lakes are also used as waterways. Among these are Lake Victoria, Lake Tanganyika, and Lake Malawi. Steamboats and motor vessels travel between ports on these lakes, carrying passengers and goods.

The Suez Canal. In the far northeastern corner of Africa is one of the most important waterways in the world. This is the Suez Canal, which connects the Red Sea with the Mediterranean Sea. (See map on page 5.) It is about one hundred miles long.

The Suez Canal was opened in 1869. Before that time, ships traveling between Europe and the eastern part of Asia had to sail all the way around Africa's southern tip. Today, ships from

*See Glossary

all parts of the world travel through the Suez Canal. The government of Egypt, which owns the canal, is now spending billions of dollars to make it wider and deeper. This is so the canal can be used by huge oil tankers that carry petroleum between the Middle East* and Europe.

Ocean routes. Ocean shipping is another important form of transportation in Africa. Ships of all kinds and sizes travel between seaports along the African coasts. They also sail between these ports and cities all over the world. Although ocean transport is slow, it is not very expensive. For this reason, it is used mainly to carry bulky goods that are shipped in large quantities. For example, ships carry farm crops, forest products, and minerals from Africa to many other countries around the world. They bring back machinery, cars, and other manufactured goods that are needed by Africa's people.

Today there are a number of large seaports along the coasts of Africa. In recent years, African countries have spent a great deal of money to improve their seaports. They have deepened harbors and built breakwaters* to protect ships from high ocean waves. They have also built many new docks and piers, where ships can be quickly loaded and unloaded.

Airways. Air transportation is very important to the African countries today. This is mainly because of the continent's huge size and the lack of good land transportation. Airplanes can travel easily to many places that are difficult to reach by road or railroad.

In Africa, airplanes are used more for carrying passengers than for transporting goods. As you have learned, air

At the airport in Kano, Nigeria. Air travel is very important in Africa. What facts help explain why?

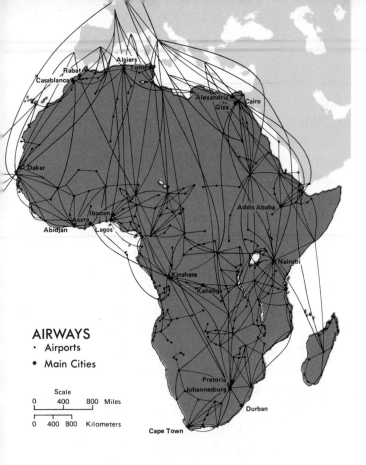

AIRWAYS
· Airports
● Main Cities

Scale
0   400   800   Miles

0   400   800   Kilometers

Airline routes connect all of the main cities and towns in Africa. They also connect the African countries with lands all over the world.

transportation is quite costly. For this reason, only goods that are very valuable or very light in weight are usually sent by air.

Since becoming independent, African countries have done much to improve their airline service. Today, air routes connect nearly all parts of the continent. A number of African countries have their own airlines. These fly mainly between the smaller cities. Major airlines from Europe and other continents serve the larger cities of Africa. They connect the African countries with lands all over the world.

Communication in Africa. In the past, the lack of good communication was a serious problem in Africa. Generally, this was for the same reasons as the

lack of good transportation. Today, the African countries are improving their systems of communication. But it is still often slow and difficult to send a message from one place to another.

In Africa today there are about four and one-half million telephones, compared to about one hundred sixty-two million in the United States. Most African families do not have telephones of their own. However, there are telephones in many public places, as well as in business offices and government buildings. Telegraph lines connect the larger cities of Africa.

All of the countries in Africa have postal service. But the service in rural areas is often slow and not very dependable. This is because of the vast distances to be covered and the lack of good transportation.

Radio broadcasting has increased greatly in Africa during the last thirty years. Today millions of people listen to news and entertainment programs on their own radios. Television is still quite new in Africa. There are only about fifty television stations on the entire continent, compared to more than one thousand in the United States.

As more people in Africa learn to read and write, printed forms of communication are becoming more important. Many African cities have daily or weekly newspapers. Books and magazines are published in some of the larger cities.

In Africa, news is often spread by people talking to each other in the marketplace. This is known as the "bush telegraph." News can spread very quickly in this manner. The bush telegraph is especially important in areas that lack modern means of communication.

Students in a medical school in Nigeria. There are not enough doctors and nurses in Africa to take care of all the people who are sick. Why do you think this is so? What are some of the other problems that are facing the countries of Africa today?

13 Problems of Development

Africa is not yet a developed continent. The map on page 146 shows that the countries of the world may be divided into three groups. Some countries have a large amount of modern industry. These are known as <u>developed nations</u>. In other countries, the growth of industry is well under way. These are the <u>partly developed nations</u>. Still other countries have little modern industry. People here produce most of the things they need by hand, or with tools that are powered by the muscles of humans or animals. These countries are called <u>developing nations</u>.

Nearly all the countries in Africa are developing nations. Most of the people in these countries are very poor. Many of them do not have enough food to eat. The per* capita income in most African countries is under $600 a year. By comparison, the per capita income in the United States is about $11,685 a year. Africa does not have enough roads, railroads, schools, or hospitals. Health conditions are poor, and about two thirds of the people cannot read and write.

How did colonial rule affect the development of Africa? The history of Africa

*See Glossary

helps to explain why this continent has not yet developed much industry. As you learned in Chapter 4, European countries took over most of Africa in the 1800's. At that time there was very little manufacturing on the continent. Many of Africa's rich natural resources were not being used.

As time passed, the Europeans began to develop Africa in several ways. They started plantations* and opened mines to produce raw materials for factories in Europe. They built roads and railroads to transport these raw materials to seaports. They also started schools and hospitals in Africa.

Today, however, many people believe that European rule did more harm than good. To most Europeans, Africa was simply a storehouse of raw materials to be used for their own benefit. They developed only the kinds of industries that had to do with removing raw materials from Africa. The native Africans who worked for European companies were usually paid low wages. The Europeans kept the profits they made for themselves.

When European rule ended, most of Africa's new nations were very poor. The situation is not much better today. Let us explore some of the problems of development Africans face today.

Economic Problems

Most African farmers find it difficult to make a living. As you discovered in Chapter 9, farming is the main way of earning a living in Africa. However, millions of African farmers are able to raise barely enough food to feed their own families. These people have not had a chance to learn about modern farming methods. Many of them cannot afford to buy fertilizer or modern farm equipment. Also, many African farms are too small to provide a good living for a family.

Many farmers in Africa practice "shifting cultivation." A farmer clears a small patch of land and farms it for a few years. By that time, most of the minerals have been removed from the soil. It is no longer good for growing crops.So the farmer moves on and clears a new patch of land. Given enough time, the area the farmer left becomes overgrown

Using
Tools

See pages 178-181

Old and new ways of farming, in Sudan. Most African farmers cannot afford to buy modern farming equipment. Do research about farm machinery in other sources, and then discuss the following questions with your classmates. What are some of the benefits of using modern farm machinery? In what ways could the use of modern farm machinery help African farmers meet their needs more easily? In what ways could it help the countries of Africa become more fully developed?

145

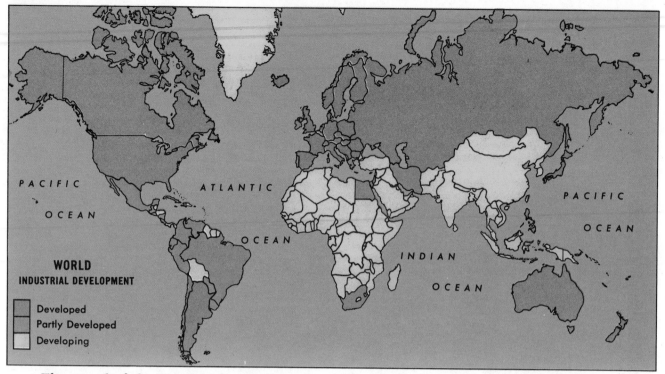

The spread of the Industrial Revolution. The nations of the world that have the most industry are known as <u>developed nations</u>. Countries that are just starting to develop modern industry are called <u>developing nations</u>. In the <u>partly developed nations</u>, the growth of industry is well under way.

The Industrial Revolution

New ways of producing goods were developed. People in many parts of the world today still live much as their ancestors* did hundreds or even thousands of years ago. But we in America live in ways that are very different from those of our ancestors. This is due mainly to differences in the way we produce goods.

About 350 years ago, most goods were produced by people in their own homes or on farms. Work was done mainly by the muscle power of human beings or animals. However, a few simple machines were in use. For example, windmills and waterwheels were used for certain kinds of work, such as grinding grain.

Starting about the middle of the 1700's, three important changes were made in the way goods were produced. First, many new machines were invented. They helped people make things more quickly and easily than before. Second, people began using steam* engines to run the new machines. Third, buildings called factories were built to house the new machines. Together these three changes are known as the Industrial Revolution.

The Industrial Revolution spread. The new ways of producing goods were first developed in England. From there they soon spread to other parts of the world. Among the first countries to adopt the new methods were the United States, Belgium, France, and Germany.

Since then, the Industrial Revolution has continued to spread. Today, it is in different stages in different countries. (See map above.) In much of the world, industry is just starting to develop. However, most parts of Europe and North America have a great deal of modern industry. This is also true of Japan, Australia, New Zealand, and a few other countries.

The Industrial Revolution changes people's lives in several ways. For one thing, the standard* of living is higher in the developed nations. Also, more of the people live in cities. People in the developed nations are more interdependent* than those who live in countries with little industry. They depend on people in many parts of the world for raw materials. They also depend on people in other countries to buy their manufactured goods.

*See Glossary

with natural vegetation and regains some of its fertility.

There are other reasons why life is difficult for African farmers. In some places, the land is too rugged or the soil is poor. Vast deserts stretch across the northern and southern parts of the continent. Some areas are covered by dense rainforests. Also, in many areas, there are often periods of time with little or no rainfall. Then there is not enough water for crops to grow.(See page 150.)

African farmers face still other problems. As you discovered in Chapter 12, some countries do not have enough good roads and railroads.When a farmer does have crops to sell, it often takes a long time to transport food from farms to the cities. Also, an African government may tell farmers that they cannot charge more than a certain price for their products. This is done to lower the cost of food for people who live in cities. If the price is too low, however, farmers may decide that they can no longer make a profit. So they will plant fewer crops and raise less livestock.

The governments of Africa's new nations are trying to solve the problems their farmers face. Millions of acres of land have been distributed among African farmers. In some places, experts are teaching people modern farming methods. However, much remains to be done to improve farming on this continent.

Industry has been slow to develop in Africa. In Chapter 10, you discovered that Africa is rich in resources such as minerals, forests, and waterpower. However, most African nations do not have enough industry to make good use of these resources.Most of the raw

A Problem To Solve
The picture above shows a smelter* in the Republic of South Africa. Although Africa is rich in natural resources, it does not yet have very many factories. Why has industry been slow to develop in Africa? In forming your hypotheses to solve this problem, consider:
1.the knowledge and skills of Africa's people
2.systems of transportation and communication in Africa
3.the amount of money available for starting new industries
4.the number of people in Africa who can afford to buy manufactured products

See Skills Manual, "Solving Problems"

Slabs of copper ready for export. African countries export raw materials to the developed nations. In return, they import manufactured goods such as machinery and automobiles. What are some problems caused by this kind of trade?

materials produced in Africa today are sold to developed nations. (See page 146.)

African leaders realize the need for developing more industry on this continent. They are finding this a difficult task, however. Most African countries do not have enough money to build factories or to import the machinery these factories would need. Also, most Africans lack the training and experience to start new industries or to run modern machinery.

Transportation and communication are poor in many places. There is another reason why it is hard to establish industries in Africa. Most African countries do not have good transportation and communication systems. This has led to a number of problems. Factories cannot be built in many areas of Africa because there is no way to supply them with raw materials. They would also find it difficult to ship their products to customers. Also, neighboring countries carry on little trade with one another because there are few transportation routes connecting them. Without good communication, it is hard for African countries to exchange ideas. In addition, it is difficult for them to cooperate on important projects, such as developing more industry. The nations of Africa are working hard to solve these problems.

Most African countries import more goods than they export. In order to make progress, the African countries must trade with developed nations of the world. By selling goods to these nations, they earn money to buy the things they need but do not produce themselves. For example, they buy tools and machinery to use to develop their own industries. However, this trade often helps the developed nations more than it helps the countries of Africa. Let us see why this is so.

The African countries are mainly exporters of raw materials. For example, they export farm products such as coffee, cacao, palm oil, bananas, and sisal. They also export minerals such as gold, copper, iron ore, and cobalt.* These raw materials are sold to the developed nations, where they are used in industry. In return, the developed nations sell African countries manufactured products such as machinery, steel, automobiles, and chemicals.

There are certain problems with this kind of trade. For one thing, the prices of raw materials in world markets change greatly from year to year. Sometimes the African countries receive high prices for the raw materials they export. But at other times, they receive much less money for their products than they expected. As a result, it is difficult for them to make plans for the future. They can never be sure they will have the money to carry out their plans.

The prices of most African raw materials have not been rising as fast as the prices of imported manufactured products. So most African countries find themselves falling farther and farther behind in their trade with developed nations. Each year, the money that they earn from their exports is not enough to pay for all the goods they want to import. Either they must borrow money to pay for the goods that they want to buy, or they must do without.

Many African countries are deeply in debt. To pay for all the goods they import, some African countries have borrowed large sums of money. Some of this money has come from foreign governments or from international organizations like the United Nations. The rest has come from banks and other lending agencies. The amount of money owed by African countries is growing larger every year. Today it seems that some countries will never be able to pay back all of the money they owe. This makes it difficult for these countries to borrow any more money.

The cost of living in Africa is rising rapidly. Today the people of Africa are facing a rapid increase in the cost of living. In some countries, prices are 30 percent higher than they were a year ago. This condition is known as inflation.

Experts say that there are several different causes of inflation in Africa. For example, several years ago the worldwide rise in oil prices caused the price of many other goods to increase. Sometimes actions taken by African governments help to cause inflation. Often a government will spend more money each year than it receives in taxes. When this happens, the government simply issues more money. Then people have more money in their pockets to buy the things they need and want. As there are not enough goods available for all the people who want to buy them, prices go up.

Today, inflation is hurting many Africans. Increases in wages are not always large enough to match the rise in prices. This is one reason many Africans have a lower standard of living today than they did a few years ago.

Social Problems

Many of Africa's people do not have enough to eat. Poor weather conditions have caused great food shortages in Africa. The rains that are needed for growing crops have come at the wrong time or they have not come at all.

<u>Droughts</u>. A long period of very dry weather is called a drought. When there is a drought, the hot sun causes crops to wither and die. If people cannot get food, they go hungry. Sometimes many of them die of starvation. A shortage of food as severe as this is called a famine.

In the late 1960's and early 1970's there was a terrible drought in the Sahel of western Africa. The Sahel is a region of grasslands along the southern edge of the Sahara Desert. During the drought, harvests were very poor in the Sahel. Countries throughout the world sent large amounts of grain to Africa to help feed the people there. In spite of these efforts, hundreds of thousands of people and several million cattle died of hunger and thirst.

Today, a number of countries in Africa are just beginning to recover from a drought that was even more severe. By the middle of 1984, more than twenty countries were affected. Some of these countries went three, four, or even five years without rain. There were no crops to be harvested. People were so hungry that they often ate the seed they had saved for the next year's planting. More people have died in this drought than in any other in the history of Africa.

<u>Poor use of land</u>. Droughts are not the only cause of famine in Africa. The people in this vast continent are not using their land well. They have cut thousands of acres of trees. This was done to clear the land for farming and to provide fuel for cooking and heating. In addition, fourteen million acres of grasslands are being destroyed each year by the livestock of nomads.* Trees and grasslands help to hold moisture in the ground. As they disappear, the land dries out and becomes desert. For example, the Sahara Desert has been extending southward more than three miles a year into the Sahel.

<u>Increasing population</u>. Another cause of famine is Africa's rapidly growing population. Each year there are millions more people to feed here. Africa has the highest birthrate of any continent in the world.

Young famine victims at a feeding center in Ethiopia. What is a famine? What are some of the causes of famine? Can you think of any ways that you and your classmates might help people who do not have enough food to eat? Explain your answer.

Millions of Africans have been forced to leave their countries. In recent years, there have been serious refugee* problems in Africa. Millions of Africans have been forced to leave their own countries and move to other countries. In 1985, for example, there were over 1,000,000 refugees in Sudan. Most of them were from Ethiopia and Uganda.

(See map on page 103.) In Zaire, there were about 350,000 refugees who had fled from Angola.

These African refugees left their homes for a number of different reasons. Some left because of the famine. Others were trying to get away from destructive wars or the rule of harsh dictators.*

151

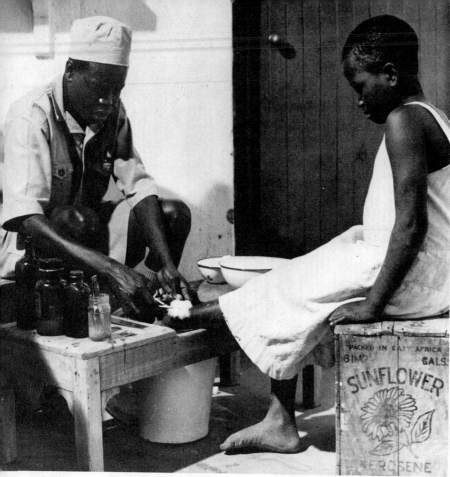

A doctor treating a patient at a small clinic in Kenya. Illness is a serious problem in Africa. Why do you think so many people here are constantly in poor health?

Life has been difficult for the African refugees. Many of these people are unable to meet their needs for food, shelter, and clothing. Many are also in need of medical care. Some of the refugees are being helped by the countries where they now live. The United Nations, other international organizations, and countries throughout the world are also helping. Billions of dollars, hundreds of thousands of tons of grain, and many medical experts have been sent to African nations to help the people there meet their needs.

A need for long-term planning. Many experts say the nations of Africa must do some long-term planning to make sure their people have enough food. They will have to take better care of their land and water resources. More modern farming methods must be used. They must have systems to trap seasonal rains and more irrigation

projects. Fertilizer, seed, and modern tools must be made available.

While Africans are working hard to solve their own problems, they will continue to need the help of other countries and organizations for many years to come. (See pages 154-156.)

Millions of Africans suffer from poor health. Illness is a serious problem in Africa. Many people on this continent are constantly in poor health. In some parts of Africa, as many as one sixth of all babies die before they are one year old. Life* expectancy in Africa is only forty-eight years. In contrast, life expectancy is seventy-four years in the United States.

Infectious diseases such as malaria, sleeping sickness, and tuberculosis take the lives of many Africans. They also rob people of the strength and energy they need to do their work well. The shortage of good food also causes illness among the people of Africa. For example, kwashiorkor is a disease caused by the lack of proteins in the diet. This disease kills many babies and small children each year.

Another health problem in Africa is the lack of proper medical care. There are not enough doctors and nurses here to care for all the people who are sick. In addition, there are not enough hospitals and clinics. Most African countries lack money to train doctors and nurses and build new hospitals.

More schools and teachers are needed. One of Africa's most serious problems is its lack of educated people. Africa as a whole has the lowest literacy* rate of any continent. (See Chapter 8.)

History helps to explain why this is so. Until modern times, writing was unknown to most of the peoples south of the Sahara. When Europeans began to take over Africa, they started schools there. But they did not build enough schools to educate all the children in Africa. Also, most schools did not go beyond the primary grades.

As you learned in Chapter 6, more than one thousand different languages are spoken on the continent of Africa. This makes it harder to provide a good education for everyone. Most African languages have never been written down. In order to go to school, many Africans must learn a language other than the one they speak.

African governments are aware of the need to build more schools. Many of these governments are spending about one fourth of their money each year for education. These countries are very poor, however, and their budgets are small. They still cannot afford to build schools for all of their children.

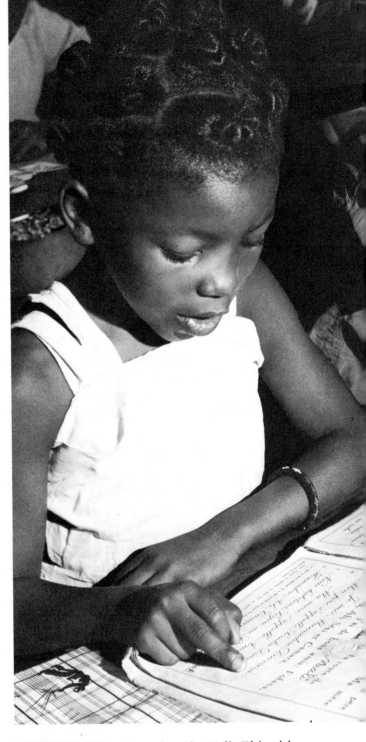

Language

See pages 178-181

A student in Mali. This girl is reading a book written in the French language. Why do you suppose this book is written in French? If you compare the maps on pages 5 and 66, you may find a clue that will help answer this question. About how many different languages are spoken in Africa today? How have differences in language affected education on this continent?

Even so, progress is being made. In many countries, the number of children in school has more than doubled since independence.

Africa's growing cities face serious problems. As you discovered in Chapter 7, African cities have been growing rapidly in population during recent years. For example, the city of Kinshasa, in Zaire, had a population of about one million in 1970. Today about three million people live there.

Rapid growth has led to a number of problems in African cities. Perhaps the most serious problem is unemployment. There are not enough jobs for all the people moving into the cities. There is not enough good housing, either. Usually the newcomers are crowded into miserable slums that often lack electricity, running water, and sewers. In these neighborhoods, there is much crime and violence. Traffic jams are another problem in Africa's growing cities. At rush hour, the streets are so jammed with cars, trucks, and buses that traffic can hardly move.

African governments are trying to solve the problems of their overcrowded cities. They are building new streets and roads. They are trying to clear away the slums for new housing developments. In some African cities, the governments are providing electricity and better water supplies. African governments are also trying to create more jobs for city dwellers by encouraging the growth of industry.

African nations are cooperating to solve their problems. Today the nations of Africa are trying to give their people a better way of life. African governments are studying ways to help the development of their countries. Because devel-

Cooperation

See pages 178-181

The picture at right shows the headquarters of the Organization of African Unity in Addis Ababa, Ethiopia. Do research in this book and other sources to discover important facts about the OAU. When was it founded? Who are its members? What are the goals of this organization? What is being done to reach these goals? Why is it important for the African nations to cooperate with each other?

opment takes time, they are making plans for many years into the future.

Many African nations believe that they can best solve their problems by working with neighboring countries. Several cooperative organizations have been formed on this continent. One example is the Organization of African Unity. (See page 73.) This organization has helped its member nations to develop better systems of transportation and communication. It has also helped to provide better health care and more educational opportunities for people in Africa.

Some African countries are also cooperating through regional organizations. For example, Ivory Coast, Burkina Faso, Benin, Togo, and Niger belong to the Council of the Entente. The purpose of this organization is to help the member nations develop their economies.* Senegal and Mali have been working together to develop the resources of the Senegal River Valley. (See map on page 5.)

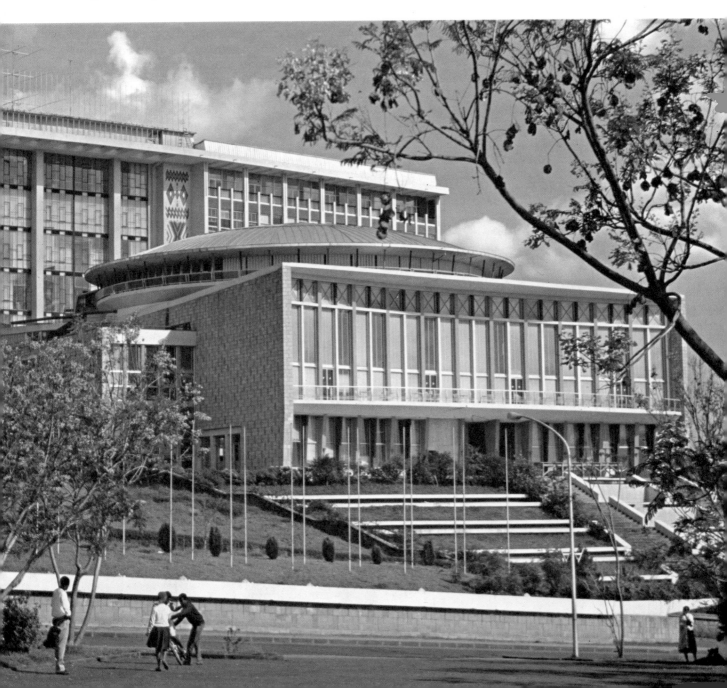

Other countries are helping Africa. Africa's problems are so overwhelming that they cannot be solved without help from other parts of the world. People in other countries realize this and are trying to help. The European nations that used to rule much of Africa are now giving or lending money to their former colonies. They are also sending advisors to help develop farming, industry, and trade. Other nations are helping also. For example, Japan is helping to develop iron ore deposits in Liberia. The United States, China, the Soviet Union, and other countries are providing additional aid. Help is also coming from world organizations such as the United Nations and the World Bank.*

The people of Africa are grateful for this assistance. But they do not want to depend too heavily on aid from other countries. The Africans themselves want to take the main responsibility for solving the great problems that face their continent today.

A worker installing communication equipment in Ivory Coast. The nations of Africa are working hard to achieve a better way of life. They are also receiving help from other countries. What are some ways in which people around the world are helping to solve Africa's problems?

Learn About Crops in Africa

Many of the crops grown by farmers in different parts of Africa are similar to crops grown in the United States. Some are very different, however. Choose one of the crops listed below and prepare an oral report about it to share with your class.

coffee	dates	pyrethrum
olives	sisal	bananas

Include the following information in your report:

1. the type of climate where the crop grows
2. how the crop is grown and harvested
3. parts of Africa in which this crop is grown
4. how the crop is used

The suggestions on pages 4-5 of the Skills Manual will be helpful in locating information in other sources.

Make Discoveries About Water Resources

Waterpower is one of Africa's most important natural resources. To discover more about the importance of this resource, form a committee with a group of your classmates and complete the following projects.

1. Do research in other sources to discover how hydroelectricity is produced. Then, on a piece of heavy paper or poster board, make a diagram showing this process. Hang the diagram in your classroom and have one member of the committee explain it to the rest of the class.
2. A hydroelectric project usually requires the building of a dam. Do research in other sources and prepare an oral report about dams. In your report, include information about the following:
   a. types of dams
   b. benefits provided by dams
   c. how dams are built
   Drawings and pictures will help to make your report more interesting.

When these two projects have been completed, discuss the following question as a class. How can the building of dams and the development of hydroelectric power help to improve the lives of the African people? The suggestions on pages 9-10 of the Skills Manual will help you to have a good discussion.

Explore Relationships

Imagine that you belong to a group of business people who want to start a factory in Africa. They have asked you to prepare a report suggesting what kind of factory they should establish and where in Africa it should be located. In order to make your decisions, you will need to consider the following:

1. raw materials available in Africa and their location
2. products you could make from these raw materials
3. possible markets for your product
4. the availability of workers in an area where you might like to locate your business
5. transportation facilities

This book contains much information that will be useful in preparing your report. Refer to the suggestions on pages 4-5 of the Skills Manual for help in finding information in other sources.

Investigate the Peace Corps

The Peace Corps is one of many organizations throughout the world that are working to help Africa and other developing nations raise their standard of living. With several of your classmates, do research and prepare an oral report about the Peace Corps. In your report answer the following questions.

1. What is the Peace Corps?
2. How was the Peace Corps started?
3. What are the goals of the Peace Corps?
4. How are volunteers for the Peace Corps chosen? What kinds of work do these volunteers do?
5. How do these volunteers help raise the standard of living in areas where they work?

Present your report to the rest of the class. Then conduct a class discussion about the Peace Corps. Ask, "Do you think you would like to join the Peace Corps some day? Why? Why not?" Information in the Skills Manual will help you in completing this project.

Part 5
Countries of Africa

A village in the country of Uganda. There are fifty-four countries and territories in Africa today.

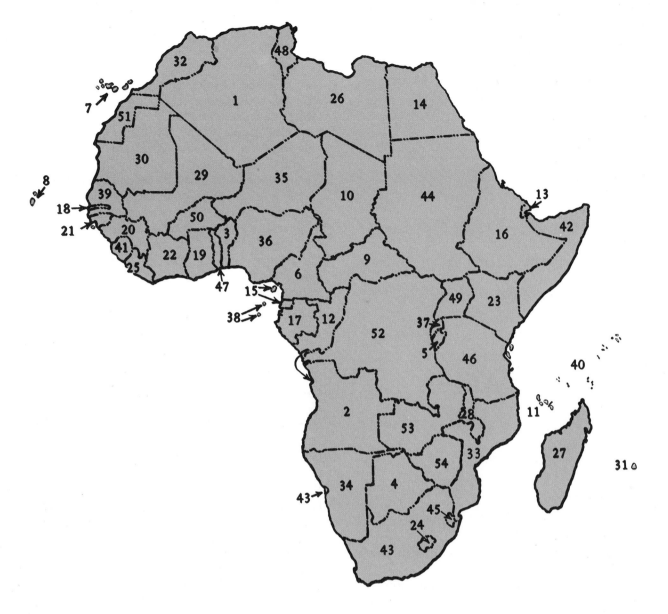

1. Algeria	19. Ghana	37. Rwanda
2. Angola	20. Guinea	38. São Tomé and Principe
3. Benin	21. Guinea-Bissau	39. Senegal
4. Botswana	22. Ivory Coast	40. Seychelles
5. Burundi	23. Kenya	41. Sierra Leone
6. Cameroon	24. Lesotho	42. Somalia
7. Canary Islands	25. Liberia	43. South Africa
8. Cape Verde	26. Libya	44. Sudan
9. Central African Republic	27. Madagascar	45. Swaziland
10. Chad	28. Malawi	46. Tanzania
11. Comoros	29. Mali	47. Togo
12. Congo	30. Mauritania	48. Tunisia
13. Djibouti	31. Mauritius	49. Uganda
14. Egypt	32. Morocco	50. Upper Volta (Burkina Faso)
15. Equatorial Guinea	33. Mozambique	51. Western Sahara
16. Ethiopia	34. Namibia	52. Zaire
17. Gabon	35. Niger	53. Zambia
18. Gambia	36. Nigeria	54. Zimbabwe

Algeria

Facts About Algeria

Area: 919,595 sq. mi. (2,381,741 sq. km.).
Population: 22,480,000.
Population Density: 24 per sq. mi. (9 per sq. km.).
Capital and Largest City: Algiers (2,500,000).

Literacy: 38%.
Main Languages: Arabic, Berber, and French.
Main Religion: Islam.
Main Occupation: Farming.
Yearly Per* Capita Income: $1,951.
Important Farm Products: Wheat, barley, oats, fruits, olives, and livestock.
Important Natural Resources: Petroleum, natural gas, iron ore, phosphates, lead, zinc, copper, manganese, coal, and mercury.
Manufactured Products: Petroleum products, metal products, textiles, petrochemicals, and fertilizer.
Currency: Dinar.
Year of Independence: 1962.

Angola

Facts About Angola

Area: 481,350 sq. mi. (1,246,700 sq. km.).
Population: 8,047,000.
Population Density: 17 per sq. mi. (6 per sq. km.).
Capital and Largest City: Luanda (500,000).

Literacy: 15%.
Main Languages: Portuguese and Bantu.
Main Religions: Animism and Christianity.
Main Occupation: Farming.
Yearly Per* Capita Income: $470.
Important Farm Products: Coffee, sisal, corn, bananas, cotton, sugarcane, tobacco, and oil palms.
Important Natural Resources: Petroleum, diamonds, iron ore, manganese, and copper.
Manufactured Products: Petroleum products, food products, textiles, and forest products.
Currency: Kwanza.
Year of Independence: 1975.

Benin

Facts About Benin

Area: 43,483 sq. mi. (112,622 sq. km.).
Population: 3,965,000.
Population Density: 91 per sq. mi. (35 per sq. km.).

Capital and Largest City: Official capital, Porto Novo (208,000). Political capital, Cotonou (487,000).
Literacy: 20%.
Main Languages: French, and African dialects.
Main Religions: Animism, Christianity, Islam.
Main Occupation: Farming.
Yearly Per* Capita Income: $230.
Important Farm Products: Oil palms, peanuts, cotton, coffee, tobacco, and corn.
Important Natural Resources: Low-grade iron ore, oil, and limestone.
Manufactured Products: Food products and textiles.
Currency: CFA franc.
Year of Independence: 1960.

*See Glossary

160

Botswana

Facts About Botswana

Area: 222,000 sq. mi. (576,000 sq. km.).
Population: 1,063,000.
Population Density: 5 per sq. mi. (2 per sq. km.).
Capital and Largest City: Gaborone (59,700).
Literacy: 35%.
Main Languages: English and Setswana.
Main Religions: Animism and Christianity.
Main Occupation: Farming.
Yearly Per* Capita Income: $910.
Important Farm Products: Livestock, sorghum, and corn.

Important Natural Resources: Diamonds, copper, nickel, and coal.
Manufactured Products: Livestock products.
Currency: Pula.
Year of Independence: 1966.

Burkina Faso   (See Upper Volta)

Burundi

Facts About Burundi

Area: 10,747 sq. mi. (27,834 sq. km.).
Population: 4,818,000.
Population Density: 448 per sq. mi. (173 per sq. km.).
Capital and Largest City: Bujumbura (175,000).
Literacy: 20%.
Main Languages: Kirundi, French, and Swahili.
Main Religions: Christianity and animism.
Main Occupation: Farming.
Yearly Per* Capita Income: $235.
Important Farm Products: Coffee, tea, and cotton.
Important Natural Resources: Nickel.

Manufactured Products: Food products and textiles.
Currency: Burundi franc.
Year of Independence: 1962.

Cameroon

Facts About Cameroon

Area: 183,569 sq. mi. (475,442 sq. km.).
Population: 9,548,000.
Population Density: 52 per sq. mi. (20 per sq. km.).
Capital: Yaoundé (375,000).
Largest City: Douala (525,000).
Literacy: 65%.
Main Languages: English, French, and African dialects.
Main Religions: Animism, Christianity, Islam.
Main Occupation: Farming.
Yearly Per* Capita Income: $675.
Important Farm Products: Coffee, cocoa, cotton, and bananas.

Important Natural Resources: Forests, bauxite, and petroleum.
Manufactured Products: Food products, aluminum, forest products, and textiles.
Currency: CFA franc.
Year of Independence: 1960.

Canary Islands

Facts About Canary Islands

Area: 2,808 sq. mi. (7,273 sq. km.).

Population: 1,343,000.

Population Density: 478 per sq. mi. (185 per sq. km.).

Provincial Capitals: Las Palmas (366,454) and Santa Cruz de Tenerife (190,784).

Literacy: Not available.

Main Language: Spanish.

Main Religion: Christianity.

Main Occupation: Farming.

Yearly Per* Capita Income: Not available.

Important Farm Products: Fruit, sugarcane, grain, and vegetables.

Important Natural Resources: Fish.

Manufactured Products: Food products.

Currency: Spanish peseta.

Year of Independence: See Glossary, Canary Islands.

Cape Verde

Facts About Cape Verde

Area: 1,557 sq. mi. (4,033 sq. km.).

Population: 365,000.

Population Density: 234 per sq. mi. (90 per sq. km.).

Capital and Largest City: Praia (50,000).

Literacy: 37%.

Main Languages: Portuguese and Crioulo.

Main Religions: Christianity and animism.

Main Occupation: Farming.

Yearly Per* Capita Income: $300.

Important Farm Products: Bananas, corn, sugarcane, and coffee.

Important Natural Resources: Salt and fish.

Manufactured Products: Fish products.

Currency: Cape Verde escudo.

Year of Independence: 1975.

Central African Republic

Facts About Central African Republic

Area: 241,313 sq. mi. (625,000 sq. km.).

Population: 2,672,000.

Population Density: 11 per sq. mi. (4 per sq. km.).

Capital and Largest City: Bangui (375,000).

Literacy: 20%.

Main Languages: French and Sango.

Main Religions: Animism, Christianity, Islam.

Main Occupation: Farming.

Yearly Per* Capita Income: $310.

Important Farm Products: Cotton, coffee, livestock, peanuts, and corn.

Important Natural Resources: Diamonds, uranium, and forests.

Manufactured Products: Forest products, textiles, beverages, and leather products.

Currency: CFA franc.

Year of Independence: 1960.

Facts About Chad

Chad

Area: 495,752 sq. mi. (1,284,000 sq. km.).
Population: 4,941,000.
Population Density: 10 per sq. mi. (4 per sq. km.).
Capital and Largest City: N'Djamena (325,000).
Literacy: 10%.
Main Languages: French and Arabic.
Main Religions: Islam, animism, Christianity.
Main Occupation: Farming.
Yearly Per* Capita Income: $120.
Important Farm Products: Cotton, cattle, peanuts, and sugarcane.

Important Natural Resources: Petroleum and fish.
Manufactured Products: Livestock products and textiles.
Currency: CFA franc.
Year of Independence: 1960.

Facts About Comoros

Comoros

Area: 838 sq. mi. (2,170 sq. km.).
Population: 411,000.
Population Density: 490 per sq. mi. (189 per sq. km.).
Capital and Largest City: Moroni (22,000).
Literacy: 15%.
Main Languages: Swahili, Arabic, and French.
Main Religion: Islam.
Main Occupation: Farming.
Yearly Per* Capita Income: $240.
Important Farm Products: Vanilla, copra, flowers, spices, and fruit.

Important Natural Resources: None.
Manufactured Products: Perfume.
Currency: CFA franc.
Year of Independence: 1975.

Facts About Congo

Congo

Area: 132,046 sq. mi. (342,000 sq. km.).
Population: 1,755,000.
Population Density: 13 per sq. mi. (5 per sq. km.).
Capital and Largest City: Brazzaville (422,400).
Literacy: 50%.
Main Languages: French, Lingala, and Kikongo.
Main Religions: Animism and Christianity.
Main Occupation: Farming.
Yearly Per* Capita Income: $960.
Important Farm Products: Sugarcane, coffee, cocoa, peanuts, tobacco, fruits, and corn.
Important Natural Resources: Petroleum, lead, zinc, gold, and forests.

Manufactured Products: Food products, forest products, and textiles.
Currency: CFA franc.
Year of Independence: 1960.

Djibouti

Facts About Djibouti

Area: 8,900 sq. mi. (23,000 sq. km.).
Population: 379,000.

Population Density: 43 per sq. mi. (16 per sq. km.).
Capital and Largest City: Djibouti (200,000).
Literacy: 20%.
Main Languages: French, Somali, Afar, Arabic.
Main Religions: Islam and Christianity.
Main Occupation: Trade.
Yearly Per* Capita Income: $400.
Important Farm Products: Livestock.
Important Natural Resources: Salt.
Manufactured Products: None of importance.
Currency: Djibouti franc.
Year of Independence: 1977.

Egypt

Facts About Egypt

Area: 386,661 sq. mi. (1,001,452 sq. km.).
Population: 47,395,000.
Population Density: 123 per sq. mi. (47 per sq. km.).
Capital and Largest City: Cairo (10,000,000).

Literacy: 40%.
Main Language: Arabic.
Main Religion: Islam.
Main Occupations: Farming and services.
Yearly Per* Capita Income: $560.
Important Farm Products: Cotton, wheat, rice, corn, and sugarcane.
Important Natural Resources: Petroleum, phosphates, iron ore, gold, salt, manganese, and waterpower.
Manufactured Products: Textiles, food products, tobacco products, chemicals, fertilizer, petroleum products, and metal products.
Currency: Egyptian pound.
Year of Independence: 1922.

Equatorial Guinea

Facts About Equatorial Guinea

Area: 10,830 sq. mi. (28,051 sq. km.).
Population: 411,000.
Population Density: 38 per sq. mi. (15 per sq. km.).

Capital: Malabo (35,000).
Largest City: Bata (50,000).
Literacy: 38%.
Main Languages: Spanish, and African dialects.
Main Religions: Christianity and animism.
Main Occupation: Farming.
Yearly Per* Capita Income: $250.
Important Farm Products: Cocoa, coffee, bananas, and oil palms.
Important Natural Resources: Forests.
Manufactured Products: None of importance.
Currency: Ekuele.
Year of Independence: 1968.

Facts About Ethiopia

Area: 471,778 sq. mi. (1,221,900 sq. km.).
Population: 35,295,000.
Population Density: 75 per sq. mi. (29 per sq. km.).
Capital and Largest City: Addis Ababa (1,408-000).
Literacy: 8%.
Main Languages: Amharic and English.
Main Religions: Christianity and Islam.
Main Occupation: Farming.
Yearly Per* Capita Income: $117.
Important Farm Products: Coffee, grains, sugar, and livestock.
Important Natural Resources: Salt, gold, and platinum.

Ethiopia

Manufactured Products: Textiles, food products, and cement.
Currency: Birr.
Year of Independence: Has always been independent except for a period of Italian rule from 1936 to 1941.

Facts About Gabon

Area: 103,346 sq. mi. (267,667 sq. km.).
Population: 1,367,000.
Population Density: 13 per sq. mi. (5 per sq. km.).
Capital and Largest City: Libreville (350,000).
Literacy: 65%.
Main Languages: French and Bantu.
Main Religions: Christianity, Islam, animism.
Main Occupations: Forestry and farming.
Yearly Per* Capita Income: $2,974.
Important Farm Products: Cocoa, coffee, rice, and peanuts.
Important Natural Resources: Forests, petroleum, iron ore, manganese, uranium, and fish.

Gabon

Manufactured Products: Petroleum products and forest products.
Currency: CFA franc.
Year of Independence: 1960.

Facts About Gambia[†]

Area: 4,016 sq. mi. (10,403 sq. km.).
Population: 800,000.
Population Density: 199 per sq. mi. (77 per sq. km.).
Capital and Largest City: Banjul (44,500).
Literacy: 12%.
Main Languages: English, and African dialects.
Main Religions: Islam and Christianity.
Main Occupation: Farming.
Yearly Per* Capita Income: $330.
Important Farm Products: Peanuts and rice.

Gambia

Important Natural Resources: Fish.
Manufactured Products: Processed peanuts.
Currency: Dalasi.
Year of Independence: 1965.

[†]Gambia and Senegal joined together to form the Confederation of Senegambia in February, 1982. Although remaining separate nations, each pledged to work toward united policies in areas such as defense, communications, and trade.

Ghana

Capital and Largest City: Accra (1,500,000).
Literacy: 30%.
Main Languages: English, and African dialects.
Main Religions: Christianity, animism, Islam.
Main Occupation: Farming.
Yearly Per* Capita Income: $752.
Important Farm Products: Cocoa, coffee, oil palms, cotton, tobacco, fruits, and corn.
Important Natural Resources: Gold, diamonds, bauxite, manganese, forests, and water-power.
Manufactured Products: Aluminum, food products, and forest products.
Currency: Cedi.
Year of Independence: 1957.

Facts About Ghana

Area: 92,100 sq. mi. (238,537 sq. km.).
Population: 13,736,000.
Population Density: 149 per sq. mi. (58 per sq. km.).

Guinea

Capital and Largest City: Conakry (765,000).
Literacy: 48%.
Main Languages: French, and African dialects.
Main Religions: Islam and animism.
Main Occupation: Farming.
Yearly Per* Capita Income: $293.
Important Farm Products: Rice, corn, coffee, fruit, and oil palms.
Important Natural Resources: Bauxite, iron ore, diamonds, and waterpower.
Manufactured Products: Alumina and food products.
Currency: Syli.
Year of Independence: 1958.

Facts About Guinea

Area: 94,925 sq. mi. (245,857 sq. km.).
Population: 5,700,000.
Population Density: 60 per sq. mi. (23 per sq. km.).

Guinea-Bissau

Capital and Largest City: Bissau (110,000).
Literacy: 9%.
Main Languages: Portuguese, Crioulo, and African dialects.
Main Religions: Animism and Islam.
Main Occupation: Farming.
Yearly Per* Capita Income: $230.
Important Farm Products: Oil palms, peanuts, and rice.
Important Natural Resources: Fish.
Manufactured Products: None of importance.
Currency: Guinea-Bissau peso.
Year of Independence: 1974.

Facts About Guinea-Bissau

Area: 13,948 sq. mi. (36,125 sq. km.).
Population: 870,000.
Population Density: 62 per sq. mi. (24 per sq. km.).

Ivory Coast

Facts About Ivory Coast

Area: 124,502 sq. mi. (322,462 sq. km.).
Population: 9,400,000.
Population Density: 76 per sq. mi. (29 per sq. km.).
Capital and Largest City: Abidjan (1,500,000).
Literacy: 24%.
Main Languages: French, and African dialects.
Main Religions: Animism, Islam, Christianity.
Main Occupation: Farming.
Yearly Per* Capita Income: $1,153.
Important Farm Products: Coffee, cocoa, fruit, cotton, and oil palms.
Important Natural Resources: Diamonds, petroleum, iron ore, and forests.
Manufactured Products: Food products, textiles, forest products, and metal products.
Currency: CFA franc.
Year of Independence: 1960.

Kenya

Facts About Kenya

Area: 224,960 sq. mi. (582,646 sq. km.).
Population: 20,300,000.
Population Density: 90 per sq. mi. (35 per sq. km.).
Capital and Largest City: Nairobi (959,000).
Literacy: 47%.
Main Languages: Swahili and English.
Main Religions: Christianity and animism.
Main Occupations: Farming and government.
Yearly Per* Capita Income: $420.
Important Farm Products: Corn, wheat, rice, sugarcane, coffee, tea, sisal, pyrethrum, and livestock.
Important Natural Resources: Soda ash, salt, gold, and wildlife.
Manufactured Products: Petroleum products, cement, food products, forest products, textiles, and chemicals.
Currency: Kenyan shilling.
Year of Independence: 1963.

Lesotho

Facts About Lesotho

Area: 11,720 sq. mi. (30,355 sq. km.).
Population: 1,517,000.
Population Density: 129 per sq. mi. (50 per sq. km.).
Capital and Largest City: Maseru (80,200).
Literacy: 59%.
Main Languages: English and Sesotho.
Main Religions: Christianity and animism.
Main Occupation: Farming.
Yearly Per* Capita Income: $538.
Important Farm Products: Corn, wheat, sorghum, vegetables, and livestock.
Important Natural Resources: Diamonds.
Manufactured Products: None of importance.
Currency: Maloti.
Year of Independence: 1966.

Liberia

Facts About Liberia

Area: 43,000 sq. mi. (111,370 sq. km.).
Population: 2,312,000.
Population Density: 54 per sq. mi. (21 per sq. km.).

Capital and Largest City: Monrovia (306,000).
Literacy: 24%.
Main Languages: English, and African dialects.
Main Religions: Animism, Islam, Christianity.
Main Occupation: Farming.
Yearly Per* Capita Income: $400.
Important Farm Products: Rubber, rice, oil palms, coffee, and cocoa.
Important Natural Resources: Iron ore, diamonds, and forests.
Manufactured Products: None of importance.
Currency: Liberian dollar.
Year of Independence: 1847.

Libya

Facts About Libya

Area: 679,362 sq. mi. (1,759,540 sq. km.).
Population: 3,608,000.
Population Density: 5 per sq. mi. (2 per sq. km.).
Capital and Largest City: Tripoli (1,223,000).

Literacy: 40%.
Main Language: Arabic.
Main Religion: Islam.
Main Occupations: Mining and farming.
Yearly Per* Capita Income: $7,900.
Important Farm Products: Wheat, barley, olives, fruits, dates, and peanuts.
Important Natural Resources: Petroleum and natural gas.
Manufactured Products: Petroleum products, food products, and textiles.
Currency: Libyan dinar.
Year of Independence: 1951.

Madagascar

Facts About Madagascar

Area: 230,035 sq. mi. (595,791 sq. km.).
Population: 10,001,000.
Population Density: 43 per sq. mi. (17 per sq. km.).
Capital and Largest City: Antananarivo (650,000).

Literacy: 53%.
Main Languages: Malagasy and French.
Main Religions: Animism and Christianity.
Main Occupation: Farming.
Yearly Per* Capita Income: $279.
Important Farm Products: Coffee, rice, vanilla, cloves, sugarcane, tobacco, peanuts, cotton, sisal, and livestock.
Important Natural Resources: Chromium, graphite, bauxite, coal, and semi-precious stones.
Manufactured Products: Food products and textiles.
Currency: Malagasy franc.
Year of Independence: 1960.

Facts About Malawi

Area: 45,747 sq. mi. (118,484 sq. km.).
Population: 6,999,000.
Population Density: 153 per sq. mi. (59 per sq. km.).
Capital: Lilongwe (130,000).
Largest City: Blantyre (250,000).
Literacy: 25%.
Main Languages: English and Chichewa.
Main Religions: Animism, Christianity, Islam.
Main Occupation: Farming.
Yearly Per* Capita Income: $200.
Important Farm Products: Tobacco, tea, sugarcane, corn, and peanuts.

Malawi

Important Natural Resources: Limestone.
Manufactured Products: Food products and tobacco products.
Currency: Kwacha.
Year of Independence: 1964.

Facts About Mali

Area: 464,873 sq. mi. (1,204,021 sq. km.).
Population: 7,996,000.
Population Density: 17 per sq. mi. (7 per sq. km.).
Capital and Largest City: Bamako (620,000).
Literacy: 10%.
Main Languages: French and Bambara.
Main Religions: Islam, animism, Christianity.
Main Occupation: Farming.
Yearly Per* Capita Income: $140.
Important Farm Products: Millet, sugarcane, sorghum, corn, rice, cotton, peanuts, and livestock.

Mali

Important Natural Resources: Salt.
Manufactured Products: Food products and textiles.
Currency: Mali franc.
Year of Independence: 1960.

Facts About Mauritania

Area: 397,955 sq. mi. (1,030,703 sq. km.).
Population: 1,812,000.
Population Density: 5 per sq. mi. (2 per sq. km.).
Capital and Largest City: Nouakchott (250,000).
Literacy: 17%.
Main Languages: Arabic and French.
Main Religion: Islam.
Main Occupations: Farming and herding.
Yearly Per* Capita Income: $400.
Important Farm Products: Livestock, millet, maize, wheat, dates, potatoes, and rice.
Important Natural Resources: Iron ore, copper, and fish.

Mauritania

Manufactured Products: Fish products.
Currency: Ouguiya.
Year of Independence: 1960.

Mauritius

Facts About Mauritius

Area: 787 sq. mi. (2,040 sq. km.).
Population: 1,035,000.
Population Density: 1,315 per sq. mi. (507 per sq. km.).
Capital and Largest City: Port Louis (146,800).
Literacy: 62%.
Main Languages: English, French, and Creole.
Main Religions: Hinduism, Christianity, Islam.
Main Occupation: Farming.
Yearly Per* Capita Income: $1,052.
Important Farm Products: Sugarcane, tea, and tobacco.
Important Natural Resources: None of importance.
Manufactured Products: Sugar and clothing.
Currency: Mauritius rupee.
Year of Independence: 1968.

Morocco

Facts About Morocco

Area: 177,117 sq. mi. (458,730 sq. km.).
Population: 23,418,000.
Population Density: 132 per sq. mi. (51 per sq. km.).
Capital: Rabat (901,500).
Largest City: Casablanca (3,100,000).
Literacy: 28%.
Main Languages: Arabic, Berber, and French.
Main Religion: Islam.
Main Occupation: Farming.
Yearly Per* Capita Income: $800.
Important Farm Products: Barley, wheat, fruits, vegetables, livestock, and wool.
Important Natural Resources: Phosphates, iron ore, coal, manganese, lead, zinc, copper, and fish.
Manufactured Products: Food products, textiles, and chemicals.
Currency: Dirham.
Year of Independence: 1956.

Mozambique

Facts About Mozambique

Area: 303,073 sq. mi. (784,959 sq. km.).
Population: 14,088,000.
Population Density: 46 per sq. mi. (18 per sq. km.).
Capital and Largest City: Maputo (785,000).
Literacy: 20%.
Main Languages: Portuguese and Bantu.
Main Religions: Animism, Christianity, Islam.
Main Occupation: Farming.
Yearly Per* Capita Income: $220.
Important Farm Products: Cashews, cotton, sugarcane, grains, copra, sisal, tea, and livestock.
Important Natural Resources: Coal, tantalite, gold, bauxite, and iron ore.
Manufactured Products: Food products and textiles.
Currency: Metical.
Year of Independence: 1975.

Namibia

Facts About Namibia

Area: 318,251 sq. mi. (824,292 sq. km.).
Population: 1,187,000.
Population Density: 4 per sq. mi. (1 per sq. km.).
Capital and Largest City: Windhoek (80,000).
Literacy: 33%.
Main Languages: Afrikaans, English, and German.
Main Religions: Christianity and animism.
Main Occupation: Farming.
Yearly Per* Capita Income: White $5,252; non-white $325.
Important Farm Products: Livestock, corn, millet, and sorghum.

Important Natural Resources: Diamonds, copper, lead, zinc, uranium, tin, and fish.
Manufactured Products: Food products and live-stock products.
Currency: South African rand.
Year of Independence: See Glossary, Namibia.

Niger

Facts About Niger

Area: 489,191 sq. mi. (1,267,000 sq. km.).
Population: 6,355,000.
Population Density: 13 per sq. mi. (5 per sq. km.).
Capital and Largest City: Niamey (300,000).
Literacy: 6%.
Main Languages: French, Hausa, and Djerma.
Main Religions: Islam, animism, Christianity.
Main Occupation: Farming.
Yearly Per* Capita Income: $475.
Important Farm Products: Millet, sorghum, peanuts, cotton, and livestock.

Important Natural Resources: Uranium, coal, and tin.
Manufactured Products: None of importance.
Currency: CFA franc.
Year of Independence: 1960.

Nigeria

Facts About Nigeria

Area: 356,700 sq. mi. (923,853 sq. km.).
Population: 91,081,000.
Population Density: 255 per sq. mi. (99 per sq. km.).
Capital and Largest City: Lagos (4,100,000).
Literacy: 30%.
Main Languages: English, and African dialects.
Main Religions: Islam, Christianity, animism.
Main Occupation: Farming.
Yearly Per* Capita Income: $720.
Important Farm Products: Cocoa, cotton, peanuts, vegetables, fruits, and livestock.
Important Natural Resources: Petroleum, tin, co-lumbite, iron ore, coal, and limestone.
Manufactured Products: Food products, livestock products, motor vehicles, chemicals, forest products, textiles, and petroleum products.
Currency: Naira.
Year of Independence: 1960.

Rwanda

Population Density: 570 per sq. mi. (220 per sq. km.).
Capital and Largest City: Kigali (150,000).
Literacy: 37%.
Main Languages: Kinyarwanda and French.
Main Religions: Christianity and animism.
Main Occupation: Farming.
Yearly Per* Capita Income: $250.
Important Farm Products: Coffee, tea, and pyrethrum.
Important Natural Resources: Tin.
Manufactured Products: Food products.
Currency: Rwanda franc.
Year of Independence: 1962.

Facts About Rwanda

Area: 10,169 sq. mi. (26,388 sq. km.).
Population: 5,795,000.

São Tomé and Principe

Population Density: 237 per sq. mi. (91 per sq. km.).
Capital and Largest City: São Tomé (40,000).
Literacy: 50%.
Main Language: Portuguese.
Main Religion: Christianity.
Main Occupation: Farming.
Yearly Per* Capita Income: $300.
Important Farm Products: Cocoa, coconut, copra, coffee, and bananas.
Important Natural Resources: Fish.
Manufactured Products: None of importance.
Currency: Dobra.
Year of Independence: 1975.

Facts About São Tomé and Principe

Area: 372 sq. mi. (964 sq. km.)
Population: 88,000.

Senegal

Capital and Largest City: Dakar (975,000).
Literacy: 10%.
Main Languages: French and Wolof.
Main Religions: Islam and Christianity.
Main Occupation: Farming.
Yearly Per* Capita Income: $400.
Important Farm Products: Peanuts, cotton, millet, and corn.
Important Natural Resources: Fish and phosphates.
Manufactured Products: Food products and chemicals.
Currency: CFA franc.
Year of Independence: 1960.

Facts About Senegal†

Area: 75,955 sq. mi. (196,722 sq. km.).
Population: 6,464,000.
Population Density: 85 per sq. mi. (33 per sq. km.).

†Senegal and Gambia joined together to form the Confederation of Senegambia in February, 1982. Although remaining separate nations, each pledged to work toward united policies in areas such as defense, communications, and trade.

Seychelles

Facts About Seychelles

Area: 171 sq. mi. (443 sq. km.).
Population: 69,000.
Population Density: 403 per sq. mi. (156 per sq. km.).
Capital and Largest City: Victoria (24,000).
Literacy: 60%.
Main Languages: English, French, and Creole.
Main Religion: Christianity.
Main Occupations: Farming and fishing.
Yearly Per* Capita Income: $1,030.
Important Farm Products: Vanilla, copra, and cinnamon.

Important Natural Resources: Fish.
Manufactured Products: Food products.
Currency: Seychelles rupee.
Year of Independence: 1976.

Sierra Leone

Facts About Sierra Leone

Area: 27,699 sq. mi. (71,740 sq. km.).
Population: 3,988,000.
Population Density: 144 per sq. mi. (56 per sq. km.).
Capital and Largest City: Freetown (375,000).
Literacy: 15%.
Main Languages: English, Krio, and African dialects.
Main Religions: Animism, Islam, Christianity.
Main Occupation: Farming.
Yearly Per* Capita Income: $176.
Important Farm Products: Coffee, cocoa, ginger, rice, and oil palms.

Important Natural Resources: Diamonds, bauxite, and iron ore.
Manufactured Products: Wood products and palm oil.
Currency: Leone.
Year of Independence: 1961.

Somalia

Facts About Somalia

Area: 246,201 sq. mi. (637,657 sq. km.).
Population: 6,124,000.
Population Density: 25 per sq. mi. (10 per sq. km.).
Capital and Largest City: Mogadishu (500,000).
Literacy: 20%.
Main Languages: Somali, Arabic, English, and Italian.
Main Religion: Islam.
Main Occupations: Farming and herding.
Yearly Per* Capita Income: $500.
Important Farm Products: Livestock, bananas, sorghum, and sugarcane.

Important Natural Resources: Uranium.
Manufactured Products: Food products and livestock products.
Currency: Somali shilling.
Year of Independence: 1960.

South Africa

Literacy: 77%.
Main Languages: English, Afrikaans, and Bantu.
Main Religion: Christianity.
Main Occupations: Farming, services, and manufacturing.
Yearly Per* Capita Income: $2,800.
Important Farm Products: Corn, wool, dairy products, wheat, sugarcane, tobacco, and citrus fruits.
Important Natural Resources: Gold, diamonds, platinum, uranium, coal, iron ore, asbestos, copper, manganese, chromium, vanadium, antimony, and fish.
Manufactured Products: Metal products, chemicals, textiles, food products, and motor vehicles.
Currency: Rand.
Year of Independence: 1931.

Facts About South Africa

Area: 440,521 sq. mi. (1,140,943 sq. km.).
Population: 32,235,000.†
Population Density: 73 per sq. mi. (28 per sq. km.).
Capital: Administrative capital is Pretoria (900,000). Legislative capital is Cape Town (1,500,000).
Largest City: Johannesburg (1,700,000).

†Does not include 4.8 million people in the homelands of Bophuthatswana, Ciskei, Transkei, and Venda.

Sudan

Main Languages: Arabic, English, and African dialects.
Main Religions: Islam, animism, Christianity.
Main Occupation: Farming.
Yearly Per* Capita Income: $370.
Important Farm Products: Cotton, peanuts, sesame seeds, gum arabic, sorghum, wheat, and livestock.
Important Natural Resources: Waterpower and forests.
Manufactured Products: Textiles and food products.
Currency: Sudanese pound.
Year of Independence: 1956.

Facts About Sudan

Area: 966,757 sq. mi. (2,503,900 sq. km.).
Population: 21,191,000.
Population Density: 22 per sq. mi. (8 per sq. km.).
Capital and Largest City: Khartoum (476,200).
Literacy: 28%.

Swaziland

Capital and Largest City: Mbabane (42,000).
Literacy: 65%.
Main Languages: English and Siswati.
Main Religions: Christianity and animism.
Main Occupation: Farming.
Yearly Per* Capita Income: $840.
Important Farm Products: Corn, livestock, sugarcane, fruits, cotton, and rice.
Important Natural Resources: Asbestos, iron ore, coal, and forests.
Manufactured Products: Wood pulp, food products, and textiles.
Currency: Lilangeni.
Year of Independence: 1968.

Facts About Swaziland

Area: 6,704 sq. mi. (17,363 sq. km.).
Population: 639,000.
Population Density: 95 per sq. mi. (37 per sq. km.).

Tanzania

Facts About Tanzania

Area: 364,900 sq. mi. (945,087 sq. km.).
Population: 21,837,000.
Population Density: 60 per sq. mi. (23 per sq. km.).
Capital and Largest City: Dar es Salaam (900,-000).
Literacy: 66%.
Main Languages: Swahili and English.
Main Religions: Christianity, Islam, animism.
Main Occupation: Farming.
Yearly Per* Capita Income: $230.
Important Farm Products: Cloves, wheat, corn, coconuts, cotton, coffee, sisal, cashew nuts, tea, tobacco, and pyrethrum.
Important Natural Resources: Diamonds, iron ore, coal, gold, natural gas, and salt.
Manufactured Products: Food products and textiles.
Currency: Tanzanian shilling.
Year of Independence: 1964.

Togo

Facts About Togo

Area: 21,295 sq. mi. (56,786 sq. km.).
Population: 3,056,000.
Population Density: 144 per sq. mi. (54 per sq. km.).
Capital and Largest City: Lomé (285,000).
Literacy: 18%.
Main Languages: French, and African dialects.
Main Religions: Animism, Christianity, Islam.
Main Occupation: Farming.
Yearly Per* Capita Income: $348.
Important Farm Products: Coffee, cocoa, oil palms, copra, cotton, and peanuts.
Important Natural Resources: Phosphates, limestone, iron ore, and marble.
Manufactured Products: Food products, textiles, and cement.
Currency: CFA franc.
Year of Independence: 1960.

Tunisia

Facts About Tunisia

Area: 63,379 sq. mi. (164,152 sq. km.).
Population: 7,161,000.
Population Density: 113 per sq. mi. (44 per sq. km.).
Capital and Largest City: Tunis (1,000,000).
Literacy: 62%.
Main Languages: Arabic and French.
Main Religions: Islam and Christianity.
Main Occupation: Farming.
Yearly Per* Capita Income: $844.
Important Farm Products: Wheat, olives, fruits, and vegetables.
Important Natural Resources: Petroleum, phosphates, iron ore, lead, zinc, and fish.
Manufactured Products: Food products, textiles, petroleum products, construction materials, and chemicals.
Currency: Tunisian dinar.
Year of Independence: 1956.

Uganda

Facts About Uganda

Area: 91,134 sq. mi. (236,036 sq. km.).
Population: 15,004,000.
Population Density: 165 per sq. mi. (64 per sq. km.).

Capital and Largest City: Kampala (500,000).
Literacy: 40%.
Main Languages: English, Swahili, and Luganda.
Main Religions: Christianity and Islam.
Main Occupation: Farming.
Yearly Per* Capita Income: $280.
Important Farm Products: Coffee, tea, cotton, sugar, and tobacco.
Important Natural Resources: Cobalt and fish.
Manufactured Products: Food products, textiles, and cement.
Currency: Uganda shilling.
Year of Independence: 1962.

Upper Volta
(Burkina Faso)

Facts About Burkina Faso

Area: 105,870 sq. mi. (274,200 sq. km.).
Population: 7,200,000.
Population Density: 68 per sq. mi. (26 per sq. km.).

Capital and Largest City: Ouagadougou (236,000).
Literacy: 10%.
Main Languages: French, and African dialects.
Main Religions: Animism, Islam, Christianity.
Main Occupation: Farming.
Yearly Per* Capita Income: $180.
Important Farm Products: Millet, sorghum, corn, rice, livestock, peanuts, sugarcane, and cotton.
Important Natural Resources: Manganese and marble.
Manufactured Products: Food products.
Currency: CFA franc.
Year of Independence: 1960.

Western Sahara

Facts About Western Sahara

Area: 102,680 sq. mi. (265,941 sq. km.).
Population: 165,000.
Population Density: 1.6 per sq. mi. (.6 per sq. km.).

Capital and Largest City: El Aiún (24,048).
Literacy: Not available.
Main Languages: Spanish and Arabic.
Main Religion: Islam.
Main Occupation: Herding.
Yearly Per* Capita Income: Not available.
Important Farm Products: Camels, goats, and sheep.
Important Natural Resources: Phosphates.
Manufactured Products: None of importance.
Currency: Not available.
Year of Independence: See Glossary, Western Sahara.

Zaire

Facts About Zaire

Area: 905,365 sq. mi. (2,344,895 sq. km.).
Population: 30,430,000.
Population Density: 34 per sq. mi. (13 per sq. km.).
Capital and Largest City: Kinshasa (3,000,000).
Literacy: 28%.
Main Languages: French and Bantu.
Main Religions: Animism, Christianity, Islam.
Main Occupation: Farming.
Yearly Per* Capita Income: $128.
Important Farm Products: Coffee, oil palms, rubber, tea, cotton, cocoa, corn, rice, vegetables, fruits, and sugarcane.
Important Natural Resources: Copper, cobalt, zinc, industrial diamonds, manganese, tin, gold, petroleum, coal, uranium, forests, and waterpower.
Manufactured Products: Food products, textiles, chemicals, cement, and petroleum products.
Currency: Zaire.
Year of Independence: 1960.

Zambia

Facts About Zambia

Area: 290,568 sq. mi. (752,614 sq. km.).
Population: 6,714,000.
Population Density: 23 per sq. mi. (9 per sq. km.).
Capital and Largest City: Lusaka (538,000).
Literacy: 54%.
Main Languages: English, and African dialects.
Main Religions: Animism and Christianity.
Main Occupations: Mining and farming.
Yearly Per* Capita Income: $570.
Important Farm Products: Corn, tobacco, cotton, peanuts, and sugarcane.
Important Natural Resources: Copper, zinc, lead, cobalt, and coal.
Manufactured Products: Chemicals, fertilizers, food products, and textiles.
Currency: Kwacha.
Year of Independence: 1964.

Zimbabwe

Facts About Zimbabwe

Area: 150,685 sq. mi. (390,272 sq. km.).
Population: 8,721,000.
Population Density: 58 per sq. mi. (22 per sq. km.).
Capital and Largest City: Harare (Salisbury) (650,000).
Literacy: 50%.
Main Languages: English, Shona, and Ndebele.
Main Religions: Animism and Christianity.
Main Occupations: Farming, manufacturing, and services.
Yearly Per* Capita Income: White $13,480; African $655.
Important Farm Products: Tobacco, corn, sugarcane, cotton, wheat, tea, fruit, and livestock.
Important Natural Resources: Chromium, copper, coal, asbestos, nickel, gold, and iron ore.
Manufactured Products: Metal products, food products, textiles, clothing, and chemicals.
Currency: Zimbabwe dollar.
Year of Independence: 1980.

Great Ideas

Ever since people have lived on the earth, they have met their needs in communities. They have found that only by living and working with other people can they have satisfying lives.

In order to make community life successful, people have developed certain ideas and ways of living. We call these the "great ideas." Let us examine nine of these great ideas and see how they have made it possible for people to live in communities.

Cooperation. In every community, people need to work together in order to accomplish their goals. Working together is called cooperation. Long ago, when most people were hunters, they had to cooperate closely to protect themselves from wild beasts and to get the food they needed. How is cooperation important to communities today? What are some ways in which people cooperate with each other? What might happen to a community if people were not willing to work together?

Rules and government. Every community needs rules to guide the ways in which people act toward each other. Why is this true? What kinds of rules does your own community have? How do these rules make life safer and more pleasant for everyone? What would it be like to live in a community in which no one obeyed the rules? ·

Fishing in Benin. These people are working together to catch fish for food. What do you think are some of the other ways in which they cooperate with one another in order to accomplish their goals? What are some of the ways in which people in your community cooperate with one another?

A wood-carver and his son, in Ghana. What do you think this boy is learning from his father? What are some things you have learned from your parents and other adults in your community?

In every community, there must be a person or a group of persons to make the rules and see that they are carried out. In other words, all communities need some form of government. In what ways are all governments alike? How do governments differ from one another?

Language. In order to live and work together, people must be able to express their ideas and feelings to one another. The most important ways of communicating are by speaking and writing. Scientists believe that all human beings —even those who lived in earliest times—have had some form of spoken language. Writing was not developed until about five thousand years ago.

How does language help you to meet your needs? What would you do if you could neither speak nor write? Would you be able to think and to solve problems without using language? Explain.

Education. Another great idea is education. In every community, the older people pass on certain ideas and skills to the younger people. Would it be possible to have a successful community without education? Why? Why not?

In early times, parents taught their children most of the things they needed to know. Today, most children obtain a large part of their education in school. Do you think education is important for everyone? Why? Why not?

Using natural resources. In order to meet their needs, people in all communities make use of soil, water, air, sunshine, wild plants and animals, and minerals. These gifts of nature are called natural resources. Would people be able to meet their needs for food, clothing, and shelter without using natural resources? Explain your answer.

In early times, people made little use of the natural resources around them. Today we use hundreds of natural resources in many different ways. How have changes in the use of natural resources affected your life?

Using tools. A tool is anything that people use to help them do work. In all communities, people use tools to help them meet their physical needs. Would it be possible to have a successful community without tools? Why do you think this?

Radio technicians in Zambia. How do you think these workers gained the skills needed for their jobs? Do you think they could do their work without using tools? Without using natural resources? Why? Why not? Do you think other kinds of work are done in this factory? Explain your answer.

Tools that have a number of moving parts are called machines. Three hundred years ago, most machines were very simple. Then people began to develop more complicated machines. These could do jobs that had formerly been done by hand. Today people use many kinds of machines to produce goods. How do modern machines help people to meet their needs more successfully?

Division of labor. In every community, not all the people do exactly the same kinds of work. Instead, they work at different jobs. For example, some people earn their living by farming. Others work in factories or in offices. Dividing up the work of a community among people who do different jobs is known as division of labor.

By using division of labor, people are able to obtain more goods than they could if they tried to meet all of their needs by themselves. What do you think are the reasons for this? Would it be possible to have a successful community without division of labor? Why? Why not?

Exchange. Whenever people divide up the work of a community, they need to exchange goods and services with each other. In this way, they are able to obtain goods and services that they do not produce themselves. What would it be like to live in a community where people did not use exchange?

In early times, people did not carry on as much exchange, or trade, as people do today. We not only exchange goods and services within our own communities but we also carry on trade with people who live in communities far away. How does trade help people everywhere to have a better life?

Loyalty. In every truly successful community, most of the people are loyal to each other. They are loyal to the laws of their community and their country. They are also loyal to certain ideas and beliefs. In the United States, for example, most people are loyal to the principles of democracy. In addition, many people are loyal to their religious faith.

To what persons and ideas are you loyal? What are some ways in which you express your loyalty? How does loyalty help you to meet your needs?

GLOSSARY

Complete Pronunciation Key

The pronunciation of each word is shown just after the word, in this way: **bazaar** (bə-zär'). The letters and signs used are pronounced as in the words below. The mark ' is placed after a syllable with a primary or strong accent, as in the example above. The mark ' after a syllable shows a secondary or lighter accent, as in **antimony** (an'tə mō'nē).

a	hat, cap	j	jam, enjoy	u	cup, butter
ā	age, face	k	kind, seek	u̇	full, put
ã	care, air	l	land, coal	ü	rule, move
ä	father, far	m	me, am	ū	use, music
b	bad, rob	n	no, in		
ch	child, much	ng	long, bring	v	very, save
d	did, red	o	hot, rock	w	will, woman
		ō	open, go	y	young, yet
e	let, best	ô	order, all	z	zero, breeze
ē	equal, see	oi	oil, voice	zh	measure, seizure
ėr	term, learn	ou	house, out		
f	fat, if	p	paper, cup	ə	represents:
g	go, bag	r	run, try	a	in about
h	he, how	s	say, yes	e	in taken
		sh	she, rush	i	in pencil
i	it, pin	t	tell, it	o	in lemon
ī	ice, five	th	thin, both	u	in circus
		ŦH	then, smooth		

abroad. Outside the borders of one's own country.

Afrikaner. Refers to South Africans who are descendants of Dutch settlers.

Allied. Refers to the United States and its allies in World War I or World War II. See **World War I** and **World War II.**

ancestors. People from whom one is descended. They include your grandparents, great-grandparents, and others farther back in your family.

animism (an'ə miz əm). The belief that spirits live in natural objects such as trees, stones, and rivers. Animists perform certain ceremonies to please these spirits so the spirits will not harm them.

antimony (an' tə mō' nē). A hard, brittle, silvery-white metal. Often mixed with other metals to harden them.

apartheid (ä pärt' hāt). A system of segregation established by the government of the Republic of South Africa. Under apartheid, white people live completely apart from people who are not considered to be white. The nonwhite people (blacks, Asians, and Colored) have few of the rights and privileges that white people enjoy. See **Asians** and **Colored.**

Arabia (ə rā' bē ə). A huge peninsula that extends off the coast of southwestern Asia. (See map, page 33.)

Arabic (ar'ə bik). One of the most widely used languages in the world. It was first spoken by the Arabs, a group of people who lived on the peninsula of Arabia. Today it is spoken by more than 120 million people in northern Africa and southwestern Asia. See **Arabia.**

Arabs. A people whose ancestors originally lived in Arabia. See **Arabia.**

asbestos (as bes' təs). A grayish or greenish mineral fiber that will not burn. It is used chiefly in making fireproof building materials.

Asians. In the Republic of South Africa, this term refers to one of three main groups of nonwhite people. The others are the blacks and the Colored. Most of the Asians are descended from people who came to South Africa in the 1800's from India and other Asian countries. See **Colored.**

Bantu (ban' tü). Refers to a large group of Negroid peoples living in central and southern Africa, and to the languages spoken by these people. The Bantu are divided into many smaller groups, such as the Zulu, Xhosa, Swahili, Luba, and Lunda. See **Negroid.**

Barbary (bär′ bər ē) **pirates.** Fierce pirates who once lived along the Mediterranean coast in northern Africa. From the middle of the 1500's to the early 1800's, they attacked trading ships in the Mediterranean Sea.

bauxite (bôk′ sīt). An ore from which the metal aluminum is obtained.

bazaar (bə zär′). In Africa and Asia, a marketplace or a street of shops.

Benin (bə nin′). A country in western Africa, on the Gulf of Guinea. (See map, page 5.) Formerly called Dahomey. Became independent from France in 1960. The name Benin also refers to a kingdom that was powerful from about 1450 to 1800, in what is now southern Nigeria.

Berber (bėr′ bər). A member of one of the most ancient peoples in northern Africa. They live chiefly along the western part of the Mediterranean coast and in the Sahara.

Botswana (bot swä′ nə). A country in southern Africa. (See map, page 5.) Formerly called Bechuanaland. Botswana gained its independence from Great Britain in 1966.

brass. A metal that is a mixture of copper and zinc. Brass varies in color from yellow to reddish brown.

breakwater. A wall built in the water to protect a harbor or a beach from waves. Breakwaters are usually built of stone and concrete.

bronze. A yellowish brown metal that is usually a mixture of copper and tin, but sometimes contains other metals.

Buddhism (bùd′ iz əm). A religion founded in India about 2,500 years ago by a great teacher named Siddhartha Gautama (sid-där′ tə gou′ tə mə), also known as Buddha. Today this religion is followed by millions of people in eastern Asia.

Burkina Faso. A country in western Africa. Formerly called Upper Volta.

cacao (kə kā′ ō). Seeds from which chocolate and cocoa are made. Also refers to the tree on which these seeds grow.

Canary Islands. A group of thirteen islands in the Atlantic Ocean, about sixty miles off the northwestern coast of Africa. These islands have belonged to Spain since the late 1400's. Today they are governed as two separate provinces of Spain. The Canaries are made up largely of mountains formed by volcanoes. They have fertile volcanic soil and a mild, pleasant climate.

Cape of Good Hope. A point of land extending into the Atlantic Ocean, on the southwestern coast of the Republic of South Africa.

caravan (kar′ ə van). A group of people traveling together through a desert or through dangerous country.

centimeter (sen′ tə mē′ tər). A unit in the metric system for measuring length. It is equal to about .39 inch. See **metric system.**

chromium (krō′ mē əm). A grayish colored metal that does not rust easily. Used in stainless steel and other products.

circumference (sər kum′ fər əns). The distance around something, such as a circle or a ball.

civil war. A war fought between groups of people who are citizens of the same country. When capitalized, the term usually refers to a war that took place from 1861 to 1865 between two sections of the United States: the North (the Union) and the South (the Confederacy). The Union won this war.

cobalt. A tough, silvery-white metal often found in ores containing iron and nickel. Used in the manufacture of certain kinds of steel and in the treatment of cancer.

coke. A fuel made by roasting coal in special airtight ovens.

Colored. One of the three separate groups of nonwhite people in the Republic of South Africa, as defined under a system called apartheid. People are considered to be Colored if they are descendants of African peoples who have intermarried with Europeans or Asians. See **apartheid.**

Communist. Refers to certain countries in which industry, farming, and most other activities are controlled by the government. In these countries, there is no democracy as we understand it. The word Communist also refers to people or political parties who favor such a system.

compass rose. A small drawing included on a map to show directions. A compass rose is often used as a decoration. Here are three examples of compass roses:

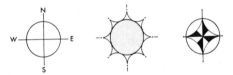

Congo River. See **Zaire River.**

constitution. A set of laws telling how a country is supposed to be governed.

continent. One of the six largest land areas on the earth. These are Eurasia, Africa, North America, South America, Australia, and Antarctica. Some people think of Eurasia as two continents—Europe and Asia.

Coptic Church. A church established by Egyptians who were converted to Christianity in about the second century.

coral. A rocklike limestone formation produced by huge colonies of tiny animals that live in the sea. Blocks of coral were used as building materials by people who lived along Africa's east coast hundreds of years ago.

cowrie (kou′ rē) **shells.** Shiny, colorful shells produced by snails that live in the shallow waters of warm oceans. Once used as money in parts of Africa and Asia.

currency. The kind of money that a country uses.

delta. A triangular or fan-shaped area of land. Formed by deposits of mud and sand at the mouth of a river.

diameter (dī am′ ə tər). A straight line that joins opposite sides and passes through the center of something, such as a circle or a ball. Also, the length of such a straight line.

Dias (dē′ äs), **Bartholomeu**, 1450?-1500. A famous Portuguese navigator. The first European to land at the Cape of Good Hope, in 1488.

dictator (dik′ tā tər). A ruler who has complete control of a nation's government. A dictator can make laws and carry them out without needing the approval of anyone else.

Djibouti (ji bü′ tē). A very small country in eastern Africa. (See map, page 5.) For a time, Djibouti was called French Somaliland. In 1967, it became known as the French Territory of Afars and Issas. Became independent from France in 1977.

Dutch. Refers to the people and language of the Netherlands, a small country in northwestern Europe. The Netherlands is often known as Holland, although this name really refers to only part of the country.

Eastern Hemisphere (hem′ ə sfir). A hemisphere is one half of the earth. The Eastern Hemisphere is the half that includes the continents of Eurasia, Africa, and Australia.

Eastern Highlands. A high plateau in east central Africa that includes parts of Ethiopia, Kenya, and Tanzania.

ebony. A tree found in tropical Africa and Asia. Its wood is very hard and heavy.

economic (ē′ kə nom′ ik). Having to do with the way in which goods and services are produced, distributed, and consumed. The scientific study of this topic is known as economics.

economy (i kon/ ə mē), pl. **economies.** A country's system for producing goods and services and distributing these goods and services to the people who use them.

Egypt (ē′ jipt). A country in the northeastern corner of Africa. A small part of Egypt lies in Southwest Asia. (See map, page 5.)

electronic (i lek ′tron ′ik). Refers to certain kinds of electrical devices such as vacuum tubes and transistors. Also refers to products that use such devices. Radios, television sets, and computers are examples of electronic products.

equator (i kwā′ tər). An imaginary line around the earth, exactly halfway between the North Pole and the South Pole.

ethnic group. A group of people who have certain things in common that set them apart from other people. For example, members of an ethnic group may all belong to the same race or they may all share the same culture or national origin.

Eurasia (yur ā′ zhə). The largest continent on the earth. Some people consider Eurasia to be two separate continents—Europe and Asia.

export (ek spôrt′). To send goods from one country or region to another, especially for the purpose of selling them. These goods are called exports (eks′ pôrts).

extinct. No longer in existence.

flax. A slender plant that is one of the world's oldest crops. Stringy fibers from the stem of the flax are used to make linen cloth and other articles. The seed of the flax yields valuable oil.

forge. A furnace, or a place with a furnace in it, where metal is heated so that it can be hammered and shaped.

geometry (jē om′ ə trē). A branch of mathematics that deals with figures such as circles, squares, triangles, cubes, and spheres.

Ghana (gä′ nə). A country in western Africa. Became independent from Great Britain early in 1957. (See map, page 5.) The name Ghana also refers to a powerful kingdom that existed in western Africa from about A.D. 700 to 1200.

great circle. Any imaginary circle around a sphere that divides its surface exactly in half. The equator, for example, is a great circle on the earth. The shortest route between any two points on the earth always lies on a great circle.

Great Rift Valley. A deep break in the earth's surface. Extends almost the entire length of eastern Africa. (See map, page 10.)

Great Sphinx (sfingks). A huge statue that stands near the pyramids in Giza, Egypt. (See picture on pages 30-31.) The Great Sphinx is about 4,500 years old. It has the head of a man and the body of a lion.

Hausa (hou′ sä). An ethnic group in western Africa. The Hausa language is spoken by many people in western Africa.

Hinduism (hin′ dü iz əm). The main religion in India. It has more than 500 million followers, who are called Hindus. These people are divided into many groups, which have different religious customs and worship different gods.

hydroelectricity (hī′ drō i lek′ tris′ ə tē). Electricity produced by waterpower.

incense. A material that gives off a pleasant odor when burned. Usually consists of a mixture made from the gum or bark of certain trees. The ancient Egyptians and other early peoples burned incense at religious ceremonies.

PRONUNCIATION KEY: hat, āge, cāre, fär; let, ēqual, tėrm; it, īce; hot, ōpen, ôrder; oil, out; cup, put, rüle, ūse; child; long; thin; ᴛʜᴇɴ; zh, measure; ə represents a in about, e in taken, i in pencil, o in lemon, u in circus. For the complete key, see page 182.

184

Indies. A name once used for the East Indies, a large group of islands off the southeastern coast of Asia. India, the Indo-Chinese and Malay peninsulas, and the Philippine Islands were also sometimes considered to be in the Indies.

interdependent. Depending on one another in some way. For example, two nations are interdependent if each one depends on the other for certain products.

intermarried. Refers to marriage between people of different races or groups.

International Development Association. An agency of the United Nations that loans money to poor countries to help them develop their economies. It was founded in 1960. See **United Nations.**

irrigate. To bring water to dry land by means of ditches, canals, or pipelines.

Islam (is′ ləm). One of the world's major religions. It was founded by an Arabian prophet named Mohammed, who was born in A.D. 570. Today there are about 600 million followers of Islam. These people, known as Moslems, live mainly in southern Asia and northern Africa.

Islamic (is lam′ ik) **religion.** See **Islam.**

Israel (iz′ rē əl). A small country in Southwest Asia at the eastern end of the Mediterranean Sea. Established in 1948 as a homeland for Jews from all over the world. See **Jews.**

ivory. A hard, creamy-white substance that comes from the tusks of elephants and certain other animals. It is used in making piano keys, billiard balls, and many other articles.

Jews. Descendants of people who settled in Southwest Asia thousands of years ago and who developed a religion called Judaism. Today, Jews live in many parts of the world. See **Judaism.**

Judaism (jü′ da iz əm). One of the world's major religions. It is based on the teachings of the Old Testament, and on the Talmud, which is an interpretation of these teachings. Followers of Judaism are called Jews. The main beliefs of Judaism are that there is only one God, that God is good, and that God wants people to follow his laws. Two other major religions, Christianity and Islam, grew out of Judaism.

Kalahari (kä′ lä hä′ rē) **Desert.** A region of desert and dry grasslands in southern Africa. (See map, page 5.)

Kilimanjaro (kil′ ə mən jä′ rō), **Mount.** A mountain nearly 20,000 feet high, in northern Tanzania. It is the highest mountain in Africa.

kilometer (kə lom′ ə tər). A unit in the metric system for measuring length. It is equal to about .62 mile. See **metric system.**

kraal (kräl). In southern Africa, a village protected by a fence or stockade. Also, a pen for cattle or sheep.

legislature (lej′ is lā′ chər). A lawmaking body for a state or a country.

Liberia. A country in western Africa. Founded in 1822 by a group of Americans who bought land in Africa to provide a home for freed slaves. Liberia declared itself an independent republic in 1847. (See map, page 5.)

life expectancy (ek spek′ tən sē). The number of years that a person of a given age can expect to live. The average life expectancy for a newborn child in the United States is about 74 years. In countries or regions where modern medical care is lacking, the average life expectancy is much less.

literacy rate. The proportion of people in a community who are able to read and write.

Madagascar (mad′ ə gas′ kər). An island country located in the Indian Ocean off Africa's southeastern coast. (See map, page 5.) Formerly known as the Malagasy Republic. Became independent from France in 1960.

mahogany (mə hog′ ə nē). A tropical tree which yields a valuable, hard, reddish brown wood.

majority (mə jôr′ ə tē). Usually, any number over half. The term "majority vote" refers to a way in which groups of people make decisions. In this system, important questions are decided and people are elected to office by the largest number of votes.

malaria (mə lãr′ ē ə). A disease caused by germs which are carried from one person to another by a certain kind of mosquito. A person with malaria suffers chills, followed by fever and sweating.

Malawi (mə lä′ wē), **Lake.** A large lake in southeastern Africa. (See map, page 5.) It forms part of the border between Malawi, Tanzania, and Mozambique. In the past, it was known as Lake Nyasa.

Malay (mā′ lā). The language spoken by several groups of people who live in the Malay Peninsula and other parts of Southeast Asia.

Mali (mä′ lē). A large country in northwestern Africa. (See map, page 5.) Also, a great kingdom that flourished in western Africa between about A.D. 1200 and 1500. (See maps on page 39.)

manganese (mang′ gə nēs). A grayish white metal. Often used with other metals to make them harder and tougher.

manioc (man′ ē ok). A tropical plant, which is also called cassava. Its roots are used for food.

Mecca (mek′ ə). A city near the western coast of Arabia. (See map, page 33.) It is the birthplace of Mohammed, the founder of Islam. See **Arabia** and **Islam.**

meter. The basic unit in the metric system for measuring length. It is equal to 39.37 inches. See **metric system.**

metric system. A system of measurement used in most countries and by scientists throughout the world. In this system, the meter is the basic unit of length.

Middle East. A large region in northern Africa and southwestern Asia. This region is made up largely of deserts. Most of the people here are Arabs who follow the religion of Islam. Geographers do not agree on the exact boundaries of the Middle East. Some of them include all the countries of northern Africa, while others include only Egypt and Sudan. See **Arab** and **Islam.**

migrate. To move out of one region or country into another, with the intention of making a new permanent home.

millet (mil′ it). One of several kinds of grass that produce clusters of grain. It is raised for its grain and for hay.

mint. A place where a country's coins are made.

missionary. A person who is sent out by a religious group to persuade other people to follow the same religion.

monarchy (mon′ ər kē). A country ruled by a single person, such as a king, queen, or emperor. This person, known as a monarch, usually becomes the ruler because his or her ancestors were rulers also. A monarch generally rules for life.

Moslem (moz′ ləm). Refers to the religion of Islam or to one of its followers. See **Islam.**

mosque (mosk). A Moslem temple of worship. See **Moslem.**

MPLA. A political party that controls the government of Angola. The letters MPLA stand for the Portuguese words meaning "Popular Movement for the Liberation of Angola."

nagana (nə gä′ nə). A disease deadly to cattle and horses. It is caused by the bite of the germ-carrying tsetse fly. See **tsetse fly.**

Namibia (nə mib′ ē ə). A territory in southwestern Africa. (See map, page 5.) Formerly known as South-West Africa. It was a German colony until World War I, when it was taken over by forces from South Africa. Since 1961, the United Nations has been trying to gain independence for Namibia. See **World War I** and **United Nations.**

nationalism. The feeling of a group of people that they belong together as a nation. Also, a strong feeling of loyalty toward a nation.

navigable (nav′ ə gə bəl). Deep enough and wide enough for boats to travel on.

Negroid (nē′ groid). Refers to the various dark-skinned peoples who have lived in Africa south of the Sahara since earliest times. These people are commonly known as blacks.

Nile Delta. The delta formed at the mouth of the Nile River in Egypt. Millions of people live in this very fertile region. See **delta.**

Nile River. Longest river in the world, about 4,000 miles. Its main stream flows from Lake Victoria northward into the Mediterranean Sea. (See map, page 5.)

Nobel (nō bel′) **Prize.** One of six prizes that are usually given each year for outstanding achievements in science, economics, literature, and peace. Most of the money for these prizes was given by the Swedish inventor Alfred Nobel.

nomads (nō′ madz). People who wander from place to place, having no permanent home. They usually make their living as herders.

Nyasa, Lake. See **Malawi, Lake.**

oasis (ō ā′ sis). Plural, **oases** (ō ā′ sēz). A fertile area in a desert, in which there is enough water to permit vegetation to grow.

oil palm. A type of palm tree that grows in western Africa. The fruit of the oil palm contains a soft pulp used in making palm oil. See **palm oil.**

ores. Rocks or other materials that contain enough of some valuable substance, such as a metal, to make them worth mining.

palm oil. A thick, dark yellow oil taken from the fruit of the oil palm tree. It is used in making soap, candles, lubricating oil, and many other products.

papyrus (pə pī′ rəs). A water plant that now grows mainly in the upper Nile Valley. The stems of this plant were used by the ancient Egyptians to make a paperlike writing material.

per capita income. A country's per capita income is the total income of all the people divided by the number of people in the country. Usually a country is considered rich if it has a high per capita income. However, these figures are sometimes misleading. For example a country may earn a great deal of money from selling a valuable resource such as oil. But if this money is distributed unevenly, the average person may still be very poor. Also, per capita income figures are often rough guesses, for it is difficult to obtain correct figures.

phosphate rock. A kind of rock that contains chemicals needed by plants. It is ground up and used in making fertilizer.

plantation. A large farm, usually located in regions with a warm climate, where crops such as rubber or tea are grown.

plateau (pla tō′). A large, generally level area of high land.

186

platinum (plat′ ə nəm). A heavy, silver-white metal that is very valuable. It is used in making jewelry, laboratory equipment, and a number of other products.

propaganda (prop′ ə gan′ də). Information that is spread in an organized manner to influence people's thoughts or make people act in a certain way.

proteins (prō′ tēnz). Certain chemical substances that are found in all living things. Human beings and animals must have proteins in their diet in order to stay alive. Foods that are rich in proteins include meat, fish, cheese, eggs, and milk.

Pygmies (pig′ mēz). A group of people who live in central Africa. They are less than five feet in height.

pyramids (pir′ ə midz). Great stone structures used as tombs by ancient Egyptian rulers. The largest pyramids are near Cairo.

pyrethrum (pī rē′ thrəm). A plant with large, brightly colored flowers which may be dried and used to make insect killer.

raw materials. Substances that can be manufactured into useful products. For example, iron ore is the main raw material needed for making iron and steel.

rainforest. See **tropical rainforest.**

Red Sea. A long, narrow inland sea bounded on the east by the Arabian Peninsula and on the west by Africa. Connected to the Mediterranean Sea by the Suez Canal.

refugee (ref′ yə jē′). A person who has to leave home and go elsewhere to escape from a war or some other disaster.

republic. This term usually refers to a nation in which the people govern themselves through elected representatives. However, some countries that call themselves republics are really dictatorships.

reserve. An area of land that has been set apart for a special purpose.

Rhodesia (rō dē′ zhə). See **Zimbabwe.**

Roman Empire. The parts of Europe, Southwest Asia, and the northern coast of Africa that were conquered and ruled by the ancient Romans.

safari (sə fär′ ē). A journey, such as a hunting expedition.

Sahara (sə här′ ə). The world's largest desert. It extends all the way across northern Africa from the Atlantic Ocean to the Red Sea. (See map, page 5.)

shadoof (shä düf′). A simple machine used in Egypt since ancient times for irrigating farmland. A shadoof consists of a long pole balanced like a seesaw on top of a post. A bucket hangs from one end of the pole. On the other end is a heavy lump of mud that serves as a weight. The farmer pulls down the bucket to scoop up some water from a river or a well. When the farmer lets go, the weight drops and lifts the bucket into the

air. Then the farmer swings the pole and dumps the water into a ditch that carries it to the fields.

sickle (sik′ əl). A farm tool with a curved blade and a short handle. Used for cutting grass and grains.

silo. A place where chopped green plants are stored for use as livestock feed. Many silos are tall, round buildings made of wood, metal, or concrete.

sisal (sī′ səl). A plant widely grown in eastern Africa and other parts of the world. A tough, white fiber used to make rope is obtained from its leaves.

sleeping sickness. A serious disease, causing fever, weakness, and loss of weight. Transmitted by the bite of tsetse flies. See **tsetse fly.**

smelter. A place where smelting is done. Also, a furnace in which ore is smelted. See **smelting.**

smelting. Melting ore in a special furnace to separate the metal in the ore from waste materials. See **ores.**

sorghum (sôr′ gəm). A group of tall, canelike plants. Some sorghums provide sweet juice for making molasses. Some are used for animal feed.

Southern Hemisphere (hem′ ə sfir). The half of the world that is south of the equator. See **equator.**

South-West Africa. See **Namibia.**

square inch. A unit for measuring area, equal to the area of a square that measures one inch on each side.

standard of living. The conditions that most people in a country think of as necessary for a satisfying life. In a country with a high standard of living, many different goods and services are considered to be necessities. In countries with a low standard of living, many of these same items are luxuries enjoyed by only a few wealthy people.

steam engine. An engine that is run by steam. To produce the steam, water is heated by burning a fuel such as coal or oil. Steam engines are used to run trains and ships. They are also used in power plants to produce electricity.

Suez (sü′ ez) **Canal.** A ship canal across the Isthmus of Suez in northeastern Egypt. Joins the Mediterranean with the Red Sea. (See map, page 5.)

Swahili (swä hē′ lē). A language spoken by about 27 million people in eastern Africa. It is a mixture of Bantu languages and Arabic.

Tanganyika (tang′ gən yē′ kə), **Lake.** A lake in eastern Africa. It borders on Tanzania, Burundi, and the Republic of Zaire. (See map, page 5.)

Tanzania (tan′ zə nē′ ə). A country on the eastern coast of Africa. (See map, page 5.) Formed in 1964 by the Union of Tanganyika, on the mainland, with the tiny island country of Zanzibar.

three-dimensional (də men′ shə nəl). Having height, width, and length.

tributary. A stream or river that flows into a larger body of water.

tribute. A payment or gift made by one ruler or group of people to another. Tribute is usually paid to show loyalty or to obtain peace or protection.

tropical rainforest. A dense forest of trees, vines, and other plants found near the equator. Yearly rainfall ranges from 60 to over 100 inches. (See maps, page 16.)

tsetse (tset′ sē) **fly.** A bloodsucking fly found only in Africa. It carries the germs of sleeping sickness and a disease called nagana. See **sleeping sickness** and **nagana**.

Tuaregs (twä′ regz). A Berber people of the Sahara. Most of them are nomads. See **Berber**.

turban. A headdress usually consisting of a cap with a scarf wound around it.

United Nations. An organization formed in 1945 to work for world peace. About 159 nations are members. Agencies related to the United Nations work to solve problems in fields such as health, agriculture, and labor.

uranium (yu̇ rā′ nē əm). A heavy metallic substance which is an important source of atomic energy.

vegetation (vej′ ə tā shən). The kinds of plants, such as trees, shrubs, and grasses, that grow in a particular area.

Victoria, Lake. Also called Victoria Nyanza (nē-an′ zə). A lake in east central Africa, emptying into the Nile River. The second largest body of fresh water in the world. (See map, page 5.)

Victoria Falls. A waterfall in the Zambezi River between Zambia and Zimbabwe, measuring more than 350 feet in height and a mile in width.

Western. In this book, refers to western Europe, and to the United States and other countries that were settled by people from western Europe.

Western Sahara. A territory in northwestern Africa claimed by Morocco.(See map,page 5.) Formerly a colony called Spanish Sahara.In 1975, Spain agreed to allow Morocco to take over about two thirds of this colony. Mauritania claimed the rest but later gave up its claim. Many people who live in Western Sahara would like it to become an independent nation.Some of these people have been fighting against the government forces of Morocco. The government of Algeria has been helping the rebels.

World Bank. Short name commonly used for the International Bank for Reconstruction and Development. The governments of about 148 countries are members of this bank and contribute money to it. When these nations need money for building highways, constructing dams, or making other improvements, they may borrow it from the World Bank.

World War I, 1914-1918. A war that was fought in many parts of the world. On one side were the Central Powers. These were Germany, Austria-Hungary, Turkey, and Bulgaria. They were defeated by the Allies. These included Great Britain, France, Russia, Japan, the United States, and other countries.

World War II, 1939-1945. The second war in history that involved nearly every part of the world. On one side were the Allied Powers, which included the United States, Great Britain, the Soviet Union, France, and many other countries. They defeated the Axis Powers, which included Germany, Italy, and Japan.

yam. A kind of sweet potato.

yellow fever. A tropical disease caused by a virus that is spread from person to person, or from monkeys to people, by the bite of some kinds of mosquitoes.

Yoruba (yō′ ru̇ bä). A group of people who have been living for centuries in what is now the southwestern part of Nigeria.

Zaire (zä ir′), **Republic of.** An independent country in central Africa. (See map, page 5.) Gained its independence from Belgium in 1960 and became known as the Democratic Republic of the Congo. In 1971, the country changed its name to the Republic of Zaire.

Zaire (zä ir′) **River.** A river about 2,700 miles long in central Africa. (See map, page 5.) The Zaire is one of the largest rivers in the world. Before 1971, it was known as the Congo River.

Zambia (zam′ bē ə). A country in south central Africa. (See map, page 5.) Formerly called Northern Rhodesia.

Zimbabwe (zim bäb′ wē). A country in southeastern Africa that became independent in 1980. (See map, page 5.) It was formerly known as Rhodesia, and before that as Southern Rhodesia. Zimbabwe was also the name of the capital city of Monomotapa, an ancient kingdom in southeastern Africa. (See pages 49-51.)

PRONUNCIATION KEY: hat, āge, cāre, fär; let, ēqual, tėrm; it, īce; hot, ōpen, ôrder; oil, out; cup, pu̇t, rüle, ūse; child; long; thin; ᴛHen; zh, measure; ə represents a in about, e in taken, i in pencil, o in lemon, u in circus. For the complete key, see page 182.

INDEX

Explanation of abbreviations used in this Index:

p — picture   *m* — map

PRONUNCIATION KEY: hat, āge, cāre, fär; let, ēqual, tèrm; it, īce; hot, ōpen, ôrder; oil, out; cup, pùt, rüle, ūse; child; long; thin; тнen; zh, measure; ə represents a in about, e in taken, i in pencil, o in lemon, u in circus. For the complete key, see page 182.

Acknowledgments

Grateful acknowledgment is made to the following for permission to use the illustrations found in this book:

A. Devaney, Inc.: Pages 112-113; page 97 by Herbert Lanks

Alpha Photo Associates: Page 147; pages 130-131 by Weldon King

Authenticated News International: Page 120

Bavaria-Verlag: Page 158 by Leidman

Bettmann Archive, The: Pages 54 and 58-59

Black Star: Pages 66-67 and 132-133

Cape Times Service — Cape Town, Republic of South Africa: Page 92

Cloete: Page 9

Contact Press Images, Inc.: Page 69 by Alan Reininger

De Wys, Inc.: Page 8 by Grevin; pages 126-127 and 178 by Victor Englebert; page 179 by Bill Kaufman

Eliot Elisofon: Pages 44 and 45

Fideler Company, The: Page 53

Freelance Photographers Guild: Pages 114-115; pages 82-83 by Esther A. Gerling

Grant Heilman: Pages 10-11

H. Armstrong Roberts: Pages 4, 24-25, 34-35, and 86-87

Harrison Forman: Pages 64, 74-75, 94, and 96

Historical Pictures Service: Page 40

Image Bank: Pages 118-119 by J. Brignolo

Information Services Department — Accra, Ghana: Pages 116-117 and 124-125

International Development Association: Page 108 by Per Gunvall

J. Allan Cash: Pages 89 and 148

Ken Heyman: Pages 138-139 and 141

Liaison: Page 100 by Robert Caputo

Magnum Photos, Inc.: Pages 26-27 and 28 by Erich Lessing; page 80 by S. Salgado; pages 84-85 by Marc Ribaud; pages 150-151 by F. Scianna

Ministère de la France d'Outre-Mer — Paris, France: Pages 12-13

Museum of Primitive Art: Page 43 by Elisabeth Little

Peace Corps: Pages 104-105 by Pickerell

Photo Researchers, Inc.: Pages 6-7 by Norman Myers; page 36 by Andy Bernhaut; page 90 by George Holton; pages 102-103 by Carl Frank; pages 154-155 by Arthur Griffin

Photoworld: Page 129 by Joseph Nettis

Rapho Guillumette Pictures: Pages 144-145 (both); pages 46-47 and 119 by Marc and Evelyne Bernheim; page 48 by Lynn Millar; pages 50-51 by Don Carl Steffen; page 121 by Georg Gerster

Sabena: Pages 136-137

Shostal Associates, Inc.: Pages 2-3, 14-15, 22-23, 30-31, 56, 62-63, 79, 91, 106-107, 110-111, 122-123, 134-135, and 143; pages 98-99 by Kurt Scholz

South African Information Service — Pretoria, South Africa: Pages 20-21

South African Tourist Corporation: Page 101

Stock, Boston, Inc.: Pages 60-61 by O. Franken

TIME Magazine: Pages 70-71 by Selwyn Tait

UNESCO: Page 153 by A. Tessore

UNICEF: Page 72 by Maggie Murray-Lee

United Nations: Pages 76, 128, and 156; page 73 by Y. Nagata

World Health Organization: Page 152

Zambia Information Services: Pages 125 and 180-181

Zentrale Farbbild Agentur: Pages 16-17; pages 18-19 by H. J. Kreuger

Grateful acknowledgment is made to Scott, Foresman and Company for the pronunciation system used in this book, which is taken from the Thorndike-Barnhart Dictionary Series.

Grateful acknowledgment is made to the following for permission to use cartographic data in this book:

Creative Arts: Bottom map on page 15 of the Skills Manual; Nystrom Raised Relief Map Company, Chicago 60618: Top map on page 15 of the Skills Manual; Rand McNally & Company: Page 1; United States Department of Commerce, Bureau of the Census: Bottom map on page 14 of the Skills Manual.

SKILLS MANUAL

CONTENTS

Thinking

One of the main reasons you are attending school is to learn how to think clearly. Your social studies class is one of the best places in which to grow in the use of your thinking skills. Here you will learn more about using the thinking skills that will help you understand yourself, your country, and your world.

There are seven different kinds of thinking skills. As you use all seven, you will become more successful in school and in life. You will be able to understand your world much better. You will be a happier and more useful citizen as well.

Seven kinds of thinking.

1. **Remembering** is the simplest kind of thinking. When you remember something, you are using information that is stored in your memory.

   Example: Remembering facts, such as the names of the earth's continents.

2. **Translation** is changing information from one form into another.

   Example: Reading a map and putting into words the information you find there.

3. **Interpretation** is discovering how things relate to each other, or how things are connected.

   Example: Comparing two pictures to decide in what ways they are alike or in what ways they are different.

4. **Application** is using your knowledge and skills to solve a new problem.

   Example: Using social studies skills to prepare a written report.

5. **Analysis** is the kind of thinking you use when you try to find out how something is organized, or put together. When you

1

use this kind of thinking, you separate complicated information into its basic parts. Then you can see how they were put together and how they are related to each other.

Example: Separating the main ideas in a book from the facts that are used to support those ideas.

6. **Synthesis** is putting ideas together in a form that not only has meaning but is also new and original.

Examples: Painting a picture; or writing something original, which might be a paragraph or an entire poem, story, or play.

7. **Evaluation** is the highest level of thinking. It is judging whether or not something meets a certain standard.

Example: Deciding which of several different sources of information is the most reliable; or judging the success of a class discussion.

Solving Problems

Social studies will be more worthwhile to you if you learn to think and work as a scientist does. Scientists use a special way of studying called the problem-solving method. In the last one hundred years, this method has helped people gain much scientific knowledge. As a result, people today know much more about the world around them than any other human beings who have ever lived.

The problem-solving method is more interesting than simply reading a textbook and memorizing answers for a test. By using this method, you can make your own discoveries. This method also helps you learn how to think clearly. It involves you in using all seven kinds of thinking skills. To use this method in learning about different countries of the world, you need to take the following steps.

1. **Choose an important, interesting problem** that you would like to solve. (A sample problem to solve is given on the opposite page.) Write the problem down so that you will have clearly in mind what it is you want to find out. If there are small problems that need to be solved in order to solve your big problem, list them, too.

2. **Think about all possible solutions** to your problem. List the ones that seem most likely to be true. These possible solutions are called "educated guesses," or hypotheses. You will try to solve your problem by finding facts to support or to disprove your hypotheses.

Sometimes you may wish to do some general background reading before you make your hypotheses. For example, suppose you decide to solve the sample problem on the opposite page. First you may want to read about the population of India. Then you can make hypotheses that are based on facts you have discovered.

3. **Test your hypotheses** by doing research. This book provides you with four major sources of information. These are the pictures, the text, the maps, and the Glossary. To find the information you need, you may use the Table of Contents and the Index. The suggestions on pages 4-7 of this Skills Manual will help you find and evaluate other sources of information.

As you do research, make notes of all the information that will either support your hypotheses or disprove them. You may discover that information from one source does not agree with information from another. If this should happen, check still further. Try to decide which facts are correct.

4. Summarize what you have learned. Your summary should be a short statement of the main points you have discovered. Have you been able to support one or more of your hypotheses with facts? Have you been able to prove that one or more of your hypotheses is <u>not</u> correct? What new facts have you learned? Do you need to do more research?

You may want to write a report about the problem. To help other people share the ideas you have come to understand, you may decide to include maps, pictures, or your own drawings with your report. You will find helpful suggestions for writing a good report on pages 7 and 8.

A sample problem to solve

Whenever you read a social studies textbook like this one, you will probably discover some problems that you would like to solve. Here is a sample problem.

In recent years, the population of India has been growing rapidly. India's government is now encouraging people to have smaller families. <u>Why do government leaders want to slow down the growth of India's population?</u> In forming hypotheses to solve this problem, you will need to consider how the rapid growth of population affects:

a. the food supply
b. housing
c. education
d. medical care
e. the supply of available jobs

The suggestions on the next two pages will help you find the information you need for solving this problem.

Learning Social Studies Skills

What is a skill?

A skill is something that you have learned to do well. To learn some skills, such as swimming or playing baseball, you must train the muscles of your arms and legs. To learn others, such as typing, you must train your fingers. Still other skills call for you to train your mind. For instance, reading with understanding is a skill that calls for much mental training. The skills that you use in the social studies are largely mental skills.

Why are skills important?

Mastering different skills will help you to have a happier and more satisfying life. You will be healthier and enjoy your free time more if you develop skills needed to take part in different sports. By developing art and music skills, you will be able to share your feelings more fully. It is even more important for you to develop your mental skills. These skills are the tools that you will use in getting and using the knowledge you need to live successfully in today's world.

Developing a skill

If you were to ask fine athletes or musicians how they gained their skills, they would probably say, "Through practice."

To develop mental skills, you must practice also. Remember, however, that a person cannot become a good ballplayer if he or she keeps throwing the ball in the wrong way. A person cannot become a fine musician by practicing the wrong notes. The same thing is true of mental skills. To master them, you must practice them correctly.

The following pages have suggestions about how to perform correctly several important skills needed in the social studies. For example, to succeed in the social studies you must know how to find the information you need. You need to know how to prepare reports and how to work with others on group projects. Study these skills carefully, and use them.

How To Find Information You Need

Each day of your life you seek information. Sometimes you want to know certain facts just because you are curious. Most of the time, however, you want information for some certain reason. If you enjoy baseball, for instance, you may want to know how to figure batting averages. If you collect stamps, you need to know how to find out what countries they come from. As a student in today's world, you need information for many reasons. As an adult, you will need even more knowledge to live successfully in tomorrow's world.

You may wonder how you can possibly learn all the facts you are going to need during your lifetime. The answer is that you can't. Therefore, knowing how to find information when you need it is very important to you. Following are suggestions for finding good sources of information and for using these sources to find the facts that you need.

Written Sources of Information

Books

You may be able to find the information you need in books that you have at home or in your classroom. To see if a textbook or other nonfiction book has the information you need, look at the table of contents and the index.

Sometimes, you will need to go to your school or neighborhood library to find books that have the information you want. To make the best use of a library, you should learn to use the card catalog. This is a card file that contains information about every book in the library. All of the cards are filed in alphabetical order. For each nonfiction book, there are at least three cards—one for the title, one for the author's name, and one for the subject of the book. Each card gives the book's special number. This number will help you to find the book. Most nonfiction books in the library are arranged on the shelves in numerical order. If you cannot find a book that you want, ask the librarian to help you.

Reference volumes

You will find much useful information in certain books known as reference volumes. Among these are dictionaries, encyclopedias, atlases, and other special books. Some companies publish a book each year with facts and figures and general information about the events of the year before. Such books are generally called yearbooks, annuals, or almanacs.

Newspapers and magazines

These are important sources of up-to-date information. Sometimes you will want to look for information in papers or magazines that you do not have at home. You can almost always find the ones you want at the library.

The Readers' Guide to Periodical Literature is available in most libraries. This is a series of books that list magazine articles by title, author, and subject. The *Readers' Guide* will direct you to articles about the subject you are interested in. Abbreviations are used to indicate the different magazines and their dates. These abbreviations are explained at the front of each volume.

Booklets, pamphlets, and bulletins

You can get many materials of this kind from the United States government, as well as from state and local governments. Other groups that publish useful materials include business companies, travel bureaus, trade organizations, chambers of commerce, and governments of foreign countries.

Many booklets and bulletins give correct information. But keep in mind that some of them were written to advertise certain products or ideas. Information from such sources should be checked carefully.

Reading for Information

The following suggestions will help you to save time and work when you are looking for information in books and other written materials.

Use the table of contents and the index

The table of contents appears at the beginning of the book. Generally it is a list of the chapters in the book. By looking at this list, you can almost always tell if the book has the kind of information you need.

The index is a more detailed list of the things that are talked about in the book. It will help you find the pages on which specific facts are talked about. In most books, the index is at the back. Encyclopedias often place the index in a separate volume.

At the beginning of an index, you will generally find an explanation that makes it easier to use. For instance, the beginning of the Index for this book tells you that *p* means picture and *m* means map.

The topics, or entries, in the index are arranged in alphabetical order. To find all the information you need, you may have to look under more than one entry. For example, suppose you wanted to find out what pages of a social studies book have information about cities. First you might look up the entry for "cities." Then you could see if different cities are listed in the index under their own names.

Skim the written material

Before you begin reading a chapter or a page, skim it to see if it has the information you need. In this way you will not waste time reading something that is of little or no value to you. When you skim, you look mainly for topic headings, topic sentences, and key words. Imagine you are looking for the answer to the question: "What are some problems faced by people in the Japanese city of Tokyo?" In a book about Japan, you might begin by looking for a topic heading that mentions Tokyo. If you find such a topic heading, you might then look for the key word, "problems."

Read carefully

When you think you have found the page that has the information you are looking for, read it carefully. Does this page tell you exactly what you want to know? If not, you will need to look further.

Other Ways of Getting Information

Direct experience

What you see or experience for yourself may be a good source of information if you have watched carefully and remembered correctly. Firsthand information can often be obtained by visiting places in your community or nearby, such as museums, factories, or government offices.

Radio and television

Use the listings in your local newspaper to find programs about the subjects in which you are interested.

Movies, filmstrips, recordings, and slides

Materials on many different subjects are available. You can get them from schools, libraries, museums, and private companies.

Resource people

Sometimes you will be able to get information by talking with a person who has special knowledge. Once in a while, you may wish to invite someone to speak to your class and answer questions.

Evaluating Information

During your lifetime, you will constantly need to evaluate what you see, hear, and read. Information is not always true or important just because it is presented on television or is published in a book, magazine, or newspaper. The following suggestions will help you in evaluating information.

Primary and secondary sources of information

First, you need to know whether the information you are using comes from a primary or a secondary source. A primary source is a firsthand record of an event. For instance, a photograph taken of something while it is happening is a primary source. So is the report you write about a field trip you have taken. Documents such as the Constitution of the United States are primary sources also.

A secondary source is a secondhand report about something. If you write a report about what someone else told you he or she saw, your report will be a secondary source of information. Another example of a secondary source is a history book.

Advanced scholars like to use primary sources whenever possible. However, these sources are often difficult to obtain. Most students in elementary and high school use secondary sources. When you use a secondary source, you should always be aware that you are using secondhand information.

Who said it and when was it said?

The next step in evaluating information is to ask, "Who said it?" Was she a person with special training in the subject about which she wrote? Was he a newsman who is known for careful reporting of the facts?

Another question you should ask is "When was it said?" Changes take place rapidly in our world, and the information you are using may be out of date. For instance, suppose you are looking for facts about a country. If you use an encyclopedia that is five years old, much of the information you find will not be correct.

Is it mostly fact or opinion?

The next step in evaluating information is to decide if it is based on facts or if it consists mostly of opinions. You can do this best if you know about these three kinds of statements:

1. Statements of fact that can be checked. For example, "Voters in Great Britain choose their lawmakers by secret ballot" is a statement of fact. It can be checked by finding out how voting is carried on in different parts of Great Britain.

2. Inferences, or conclusions that are based on facts. The statement "The people of Great Britain live in a democracy" is an inference. This inference is based on the fact that British citizens choose their lawmakers by secret ballot, and on other facts that can be proved. It is important to remember that inferences can be false or only partly true, even though they are based on facts.

3. Value judgments, or opinions. The statement "It is always wrong for a country to go to war" is a value judgment. Since a value judgment is an opinion, you need to look at it very carefully. On what facts and inferences is it based? What facts and conclusions do you think form the basis of the opinion, "It is always wrong for a country to go to war"? Do you agree or disagree with these conclusions? Trustworthy writers let their readers know which statements are their own opinions. They also try to base their opinions as much as possible on facts that can be proved.

Why was it said?

The next step in evaluating information is to find out the purpose for which it was prepared. Many books and articles are prepared in an honest effort to give correct information. Scientists writing about new discoveries will generally try to report their findings as accurately as possible. They will be careful to distinguish between things they have actually seen and conclusions they have drawn from their observations.

Some information, however, is prepared mostly to persuade people to believe or act a certain way. Information of this kind is called propaganda.

Some propaganda is used to promote causes that are generally thought to be good. A picture that shows Smokey the Bear and the words "Only you can prevent forest fires" is an example of this kind of propaganda.

Propaganda is also used to make people support causes they would not agree with if they knew more about them. This kind of propaganda may be made up of information that is true, partly true, or false. Even when it is true, however, the information may be presented in such a way as to mislead you.

Propaganda generally appeals to people's feelings rather than to their thinking ability. For this reason, you should learn to recognize information that is propaganda. Then you can think about it calmly and clearly, and evaluate it wisely.

Making Reports

There are many times when you need to share information or ideas with others. Sometimes you will need to do this in writing. Other times you will need to do it by speaking. One of the best ways to develop your writing and speaking skills is by making written and oral reports. The success of your report will depend on how well you have organized your material. It will also depend on your skill in presenting it. Here are some guidelines that will help you in preparing a good report.

Decide upon a goal

Have your goal clearly in mind. Are you mostly interested in sharing information? Do you want to give your own ideas on a subject? Or are you trying to persuade other people to agree with you?

Find the information you need

Be sure to use more than one source. If you are not sure how to find information about your subject, read the suggestions on pages 4 and 5.

Take good notes

To remember what you have read, you must take notes. Before you begin taking notes, however, you will need to make a list of the questions you want your report to answer. As you do research, write down the facts that answer these questions. You may find some interesting and important facts that do not answer any of your questions. If you feel that they might be useful in your report, write them down, too. Your notes should be short and in your own words except when you want to use quotations. When you use an exact quotation, be sure to put quotation marks around it.

You will be able to make the best use of your notes if you write them on file cards. Use a separate card for each statement or group of statements that answers one of your questions. To remember where your information came from, write on each card the title, author, and date of the source. When you have finished taking notes, group the cards according to the questions they answer.

Make an outline

After you have reviewed your notes, make an outline. This is a general plan that shows the order and the relationship of the ideas you want to include in your report. The first step in making an outline is to pick out the main ideas. These will be the main headings in your outline. (See sample outline on page 8.) Next, list under each of these headings the ideas and facts that support or explain it. As you arrange your information, ask yourself the following questions.

a. Is there one main idea I must put first because everything else depends on this idea?
b. Have I arranged my facts in such a way as to show how they are related to one another?

c. Are there some ideas that will be clearer if they come after other ideas have been explained?

d. Have I included enough facts so that I can end my outline with a summary statement or a logical conclusion?

When you have finished your first outline, you may find that some parts of it are too short. If so, you may wish to do more research. When you feel that you have enough information, make your final outline. Remember that this outline will serve as a guide for your finished report.

Example of an outline

The author of this Skills Manual prepared the following outline before writing "Making Reports."

I. Introduction
II. Deciding upon a goal
III. Finding information
IV. Taking notes
   A. List main ideas to be researched
   B. Write on file cards facts that support or explain these ideas
   C. Group cards according to main ideas
V. Making an outline
   A. Purpose of an outline
   B. Guidelines for arranging information
   C. Sample outline of this section
VI. Preparing a written report
VII. Presenting an oral report

Special guidelines for a written report

Using your outline as a guide, write your report. The following suggestions will help you to make your report interesting and clear.

Create word pictures that your readers can see in their minds. Before you begin, imagine that you are going to make a movie of the subject you plan to write about. What scenes would you like to show? Next, think of the words that will bring these same pictures into your readers' minds.

Group your sentences into good paragraphs. It is generally best to begin a paragraph with a topic sentence that says to the reader, "This is what you will learn about in this paragraph." The other sentences in the paragraph should help to support or explain the topic sentence.

A sample paragraph. Below is a sample paragraph from a textbook about South America. The topic sentence has been underlined. Notice how clear it is and how well the other sentences support it. Also notice how many pictures the paragraph puts in your mind.

The Pampa of Argentina is one of the best wheat-growing areas of the world. At harvest-time, thousands of acres of golden grain stretch out across the land. The hot summers and rich soil of this area provide excellent conditions for growing grain. During the harvest season large combines move through the wheat fields, cutting and threshing the grain as they go. Some of the farmers also grow other grains such as corn, oats, and barley.

Other guidelines. There are two other things to remember in writing a good report. First, use the dictionary to find the spelling of words you are not sure about. Second, make a list of the sources of information you used. Put this list at the beginning or end of your report. This list is called a bibliography.

Special guidelines for an oral report

When you are going to give a report orally, you will also want to arrange your information in a logical order by making an outline. Prepare notes to guide you during your talk. These notes should be complete enough to help you remember all the points you want to make. You may even write out certain parts of your report that you would rather read.

When you present your report, speak directly to your audience. Pronounce your words correctly and clearly. Remember to speak slowly enough for your listeners to follow what you are saying. Use a tone of voice that will hold their interest. Stand up straight, but try not to be too stiff. Remember, the only way to improve your speaking skills is to practice them correctly.

Holding a Group Discussion

One of the important ways in which you learn is by exchanging ideas with other people. You do this often in everyday conversation. You are likely to learn more, however, when you take part in the special kind of group conversation that we call a discussion. A discussion is more orderly than a conversation. It generally has a definite, serious purpose. This purpose may be the sharing of information or the solving of a problem. In order to reach its goal, the discussion group must arrive at a conclusion or make a decision of some kind.

The guidelines below will help you to have a successful discussion.

Be prepared

Think about the subject to be discussed ahead of time. Prepare for the discussion by reading and taking notes. You may also want to make an outline of the ideas you want to share with the group.

Take part

Take part in the discussion. Express your ideas clearly and in as few words as possible. Be sure that the statements you make and the questions you ask deal with the subject being talked about.

Listen and think

Listen thoughtfully to others. Encourage all of the members of the discussion group to express their ideas. Do not make up your mind about a question or a problem until all of the facts have been given.

Be courteous

When you speak, address the whole group. Ask and answer questions politely. When you do not agree with someone, give your reasons in a friendly way.

Working With Others

In school and throughout life, you will find that there are many things that can be done better by a group than by one person working alone. Some of these projects would take too long to finish if they were done by one person. Others have different parts that can be done best by people with different talents.

Before your group begins a project, you should decide several matters. First, decide exactly what goal you are trying to reach. Second, decide what part of the project each person should do. Third, decide when the project is to be finished.

Do your part

Remember that the success of your project depends on every member of the group. Be willing to do your share of the work and to accept your share of the responsibility.

Follow the rules

Help the group decide on reasonable rules. Then follow them. When a difference of opinion cannot be settled by discussion, make a decision by majority* vote.

Share your ideas

Be willing to share your ideas with the group. When you present an idea for discussion, be prepared to see it criticized or even rejected. At the same time, have the courage to stand up for an idea or a belief that is really important to you.

Be friendly, thoughtful, helpful, cheerful

Try to express your opinions seriously and sincerely without hurting others or losing their respect. Listen politely to the ideas of others.

*See Glossary

Learn from your mistakes

Look for ways in which you can be a better group member the next time you work with others on a project.

Building Your Vocabulary

When you do research in many different kinds of reading materials, you are likely to find several words you have never seen before. If you skip over these words, you may not fully understand what you are reading. The following suggestions will help you to discover the meanings of new words and build your vocabulary.

1. See how the word is used in the sentence. When you come to a new word, don't stop reading. Read on beyond the new word to see if you can discover any hints as to what its meaning might be. Trying to figure out the meaning of a word from the way it is used may not give you the exact definition. However, it will give you a general idea of what the word means.

2. Sound out the word. Break the word up into syllables, and try to pronounce it. When you say the word aloud, you may find that you know it after all but have simply never seen it in print.

3. Look in the dictionary. When you think you have figured out what a word means and how it is pronounced, look it up in the dictionary. First, check the pronunciation. Have you pronounced it correctly? Then, check the meaning of the word. Remember, most words have more than one meaning. Did you decide on the right definition?

4. Make a list of the new words you learn. In your own words, write a definition of each word you place on your list. Review this list from time to time.

Learning Map Skills

The earth is a sphere

Our earth is round like a ball. We call anything with this shape a sphere. The earth is, of course, a very large sphere. Its diameter* is about 8,000 miles (12,874 kilometers*). Its circumference* is about 25,000 miles (40,233 kilometers). The earth is not quite a perfect sphere. It is somewhat flat at the North and South poles.

Globes and maps

The globe in your classroom is also a sphere. It is a small-size copy of the earth. The surface of the globe shows the shapes of the areas of land on the earth. It also shows the shapes of the different bodies of water. By looking at the globe, you can see exactly where the continents, islands, and oceans are. Globes are made with the North Pole at the top. But they are often tipped to show the way the earth is tipped. Maps are flat drawings. They may show part or all of the earth's surface.

Scale

Globes and maps give information about distance. When you use them, you need to know what distance on the earth is represented by a given distance on the globe or map. This relationship is called the scale. The scale of a globe or map may be shown in several different ways.

On most maps, the scale is shown by a small drawing. For example:

Scale
```
0        200      400 Miles
|----------|----------|
0        322      644 Kilometers
```

Sometimes, the scale is shown in this way: 1 inch = 400 miles (644 kilometers).

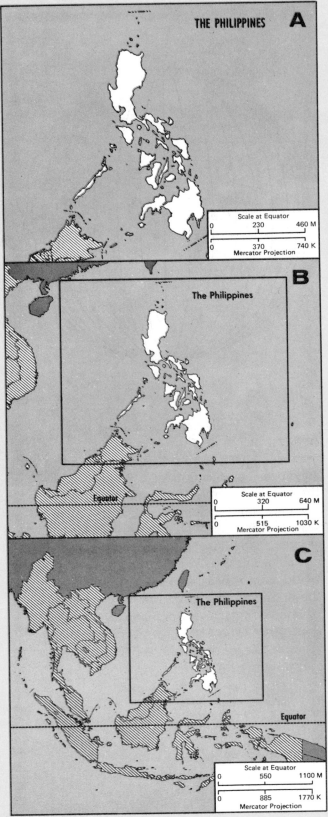

The Philippines is a different size on each of the three maps above. This is because one inch on each of these maps represents a different distance on the surface of the earth.

Finding places on the earth

People have always wanted to know just where certain places are located on the earth. Over the years, a very accurate way of giving such information has been worked out. This system is used all over the world.

In order to work out a means of finding anything, you need starting points and a measuring unit. The North and South poles and the equator* are the starting points for the system we use to find places on the earth. The measuring unit for our system is called the degree (°).

Parallels show latitude

When we want to find a place on the earth, we first find out how far it is north or south of the equator. This distance measured in degrees is called north or south latitude. The equator stands for zero latitude. The North Pole is located at 90 degrees north latitude. The South Pole is at 90 degrees south latitude.

All points on the earth that have the same latitude are the same distance from the equator. A line connecting such points is called a parallel. This is because it is parallel to the equator. (See globe D on the next page.)

Meridians show longitude

After we know the latitude of a place, we need to know its location in an east-west direction. This is called its longitude. The lines that show longitude are called meridians. They are drawn so as to connect the North and South poles (See globe E on the next page.) Longitude is measured from the meridian that passes through Greenwich, England. This line of zero longitude is called the prime meridian. Distance east or west of this meridian, measured in degrees, is called east or west longitude. The meridian of 180 degrees west longitude is the same as the one of 180 degrees east longitude. This is because 180 degrees is exactly halfway around the world from the prime meridian.

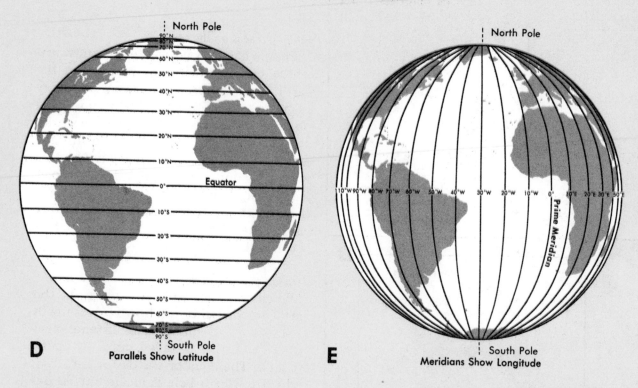

North Pole

D
Parallels Show Latitude
South Pole

North Pole

E
Meridians Show Longitude
South Pole

Finding places on a globe

The location of a certain place might be given to you like this: 30° N 90° W. This means that this place is located 30 degrees north of the equator, and 90 degrees west of the prime meridian. See if you can find this place on the globe in your classroom. It is helpful to remember that parallels and meridians are drawn every ten or fifteen degrees on most globes.

The round earth on a flat map

An important fact about a sphere is that you cannot flatten out its surface perfectly. To prove this, you might do the following. Cut an orange in half. Scrape away the fruit. You will not be able to press either piece of orange peel flat without crushing it. If you cut one piece in half, however, you can press these smaller pieces nearly flat. Next, cut one of these pieces of peel into three smaller pieces, shaped like those in drawing F on the opposite page. You will be able to press these pieces quite flat.

A map like the one shown in drawing F can be made by cutting the surface of a globe into twelve pieces shaped like the smallest pieces of your orange peel. Such a map would be accurate. However, an "orange-peel" map is not easy to use, because the continents and oceans are cut apart.

A flat map can never show the earth's surface as truthfully as a globe can. On globes, shape, size, distance, and direction are all accurate. A single flat map of the world cannot be drawn to show all four of these things correctly. But flat maps can be made that show some of these things accurately. The different ways of drawing maps of the world to show different things correctly are called map projections.

The Mercator projection

Drawing G, on the opposite page, shows a world map called a Mercator projection. When you compare this map with a globe, you can see that continents, islands, and oceans have almost the right shape. On this kind of map, however, North America seems larger than Africa. This is not true. On Mercator maps, lands far from the equator appear larger than they are.

Because they show true directions, Mercator maps are very useful to sailors and fliers. For instance, the city of Lisbon, Portugal, lies almost exactly east of Baltimore, Maryland. A Mercator map shows that a ship could reach Lisbon by sailing from Baltimore straight east across the Atlantic Ocean. A plane could also reach Lisbon by flying straight east from Baltimore.

The shortest route

Strangely enough, the best way to reach Lisbon from Baltimore is not by going straight east. There is a shorter route. In order to understand why this is so, you might like to do the following.

On your classroom globe, find Lisbon and Baltimore. Both cities lie just south of the 40th parallel. Take a piece of string and connect the two cities. Let the string follow the true east-west direction of the 40th parallel. Now, draw the string tight. Notice that it passes far to the north of the 40th parallel. The path of the tightened string is the shortest route between Baltimore and Lisbon. The shortest route between any two points on the earth is called the great* circle route.

A Round Globe on a Flat Surface

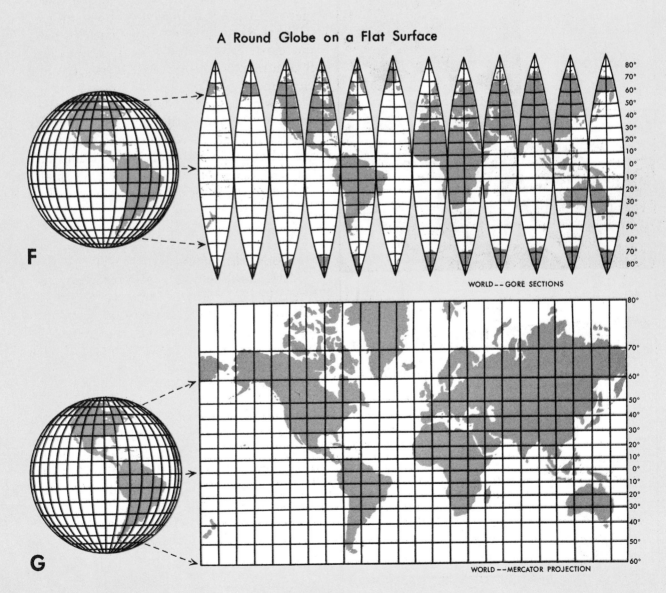

F

WORLD -- GORE SECTIONS

G

WORLD -- MERCATOR PROJECTION

13

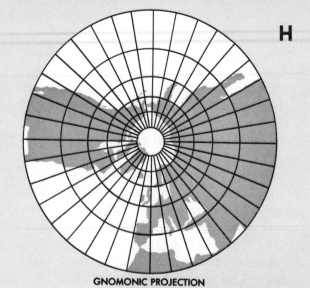

GNOMONIC PROJECTION

H

The gnomonic (nō mon′ ik) projection

Using a globe and a piece of string is not a very handy or accurate way of finding great circle routes. Instead, sailors and fliers use a special kind of map called the gnomonic projection. (See drawing H, at left.) On this kind of map, the great circle route between any two places can be found simply by drawing a straight line between them.

Special-Purpose Maps

Maps that show part of the earth

For some uses, we would rather have maps that do not show the whole surface of the earth. A map of a very small part of the earth can be drawn more accurately than a map of a large area. It can also include more details.

Drawing I, on this page, shows a photograph and a map of the same small part of the earth. The drawings on the map that show the shape and location of things on the earth are called symbols. The small drawing that shows directions is called a compass* rose.

Maps for special purposes

Maps can show the location of many different kinds of things. For instance, a map can show what minerals are found in certain places, or what crops are grown. A small chart that lists the symbols and their meanings is usually included on a map. This is called the key.

Symbols on some geography maps stand for the amounts of things in different places. For instance, map J, at left, gives information about the number of people in the southwestern part of the United States. The key tells the meaning of the symbols. In this case the symbols are dots and circles.

On different maps, the same symbol may stand for different things and amounts.

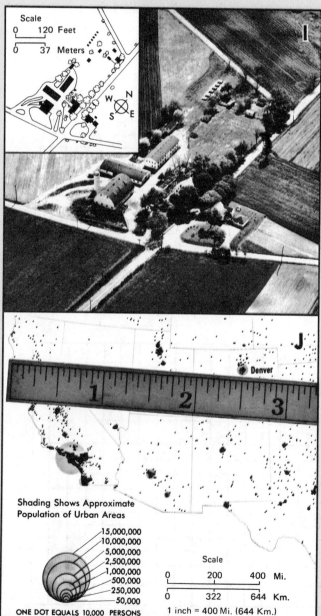

I

J

14

Each dot on map J stands for 10,000 persons. On other maps, a dot might represent 5,000 sheep or 1,000 bushels of wheat.

There are other ways of giving information about quantity. For example, different designs may be used on a rainfall map to show the areas that receive different amounts of rain each year.

Relief Maps

The roughness of the earth's surface

From a plane, you can see that the earth's surface is rough. You can see mountains and valleys, hills and plains. For some purposes, globes and maps that show these things are needed. They are called relief globes and maps.

Since globes are copies of the earth, you may wonder why most globes do not show the roughness of the earth's surface. The reason for this is that even the highest mountain on the earth is not very large when it is compared with the earth's diameter. Even a very large globe would be smooth nearly everywhere.

In order to make a relief globe or map, you must use a different scale for the height of the land. You might start with a large flat map. One inch on your flat map may stand for a distance of 100 miles (161 kilometers) on the earth. Now you are going to make a small copy of a mountain on your map. On the earth, this mountain is two miles (3.2 kilometers) high. If you let one inch stand for this height on the earth, your mountain should rise one inch above the flat surface of your map. Other mountains and hills should be copied on this same scale.

By photographing relief globes and maps, flat maps can be made that show the earth much as it looks from an airplane. Map K, at right above, is a photograph of a relief map. Map L is a photograph of a relief globe.

Topographic maps

Another kind of map that shows the roughness of the earth's surface is called a topographic, or contour, map. On this kind of map, lines are drawn to show how high the land rises above sea level. These are

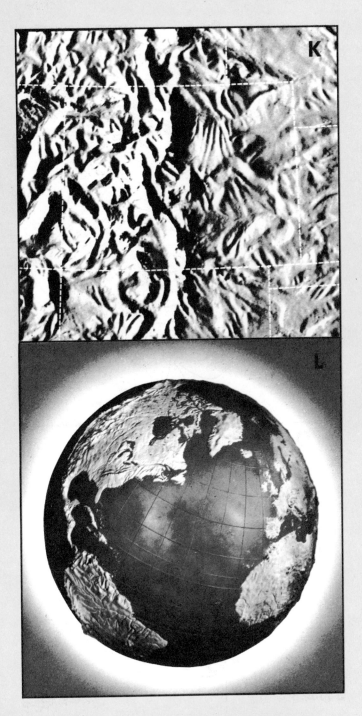

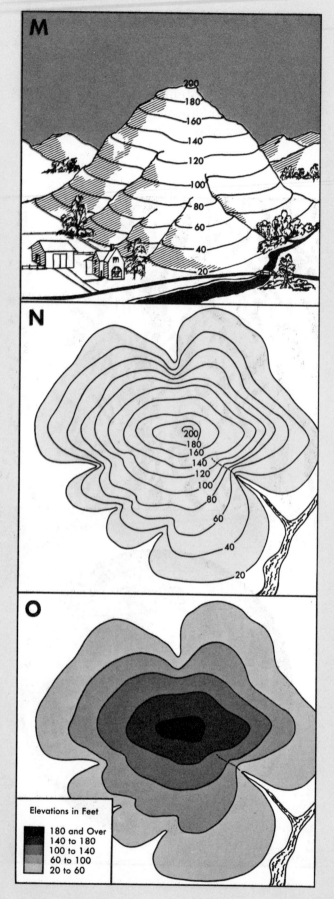

called contour lines. The drawings on this page help to explain how topographic maps are made.

Map M is a drawing of a hill. Around the bottom of the hill is our first contour line. This line connects all the points at the base of the hill that are exactly twenty feet above sea level. Higher up the hill, another contour line is drawn. It connects all the points that are exactly forty feet above sea level. A line is also drawn at a height of sixty feet. Other lines are drawn every twenty feet until the top of the hill is reached. Since the hill is shaped somewhat like a cone, each contour line is shorter than the one just below it.

Map N shows how the contour lines in the drawing of the hill M can be used to make a topographic map. This map gives us a great deal of information about the hill. Since each line is labeled with the height it stands for, you can tell how high the different parts of the hill are. It is important to remember that land does not really rise in layers, as you might think when you look at a topographic map. Wherever the contour lines are far apart, you can be sure that the land slopes gently. Where they are close together, the slope is steep. With practice, you can picture the land in your mind as you look at such a map. Topographic maps are especially useful to people who design such things as roads and buildings.

On a topographic map, the spaces between the contour lines may be filled in with different shades of a color. If a different shade of brown were used for each different height of land shown in map N, there would be ten shades. It would be very hard for you to tell these different shades of brown apart. Therefore, on map O, at left, black and four shades of brown were used to show differences in height of forty feet. The key shows the height of the land represented by the different shades. On some topographic maps, different colors are used to stand for different heights.